SECRET POLICE

Other books by Peter Benjaminson

SECRET POLICE

Inside the New York City
Department of Investigation

PETER BENJAMINSON

BARRICADE BOOKS INC. / New York

Published by Barricade Books Inc.
150 Fifth Avenue
New York, NY 10011

Copyright © 1997 by Peter Benjaminson

Printed in the United States of America.

Library of Congress Cataloging-in-Publication Data

Benjaminson, Peter, 1945–
        Secret police : inside the Department of Investigation / by Peter
    Benjaminson.
            p.   cm.
        ISBN 1-56980-090-1
            1. Political corruption—New York (State)—New York.
        2. Corruption investigation—New York (State)—New York.
        3. Undercover operations—New York (State)—New York.
        4. New York (N.Y.). Dept. of Investigation.   I. Title.
        JS1239.B46 1996
        364. 1'31'097471—dc20   96-24933
                                                                CIP

10 9 8 7 6 5 4 3 2 1

To the people in this
book whose names have
been changed. You know
who you are and what
you have done.

THANKS . . .

I can't thank anyone currently or recently at DOI for their help, by name. (Neither the presence nor absence of a DOI employee's or former employee's name in this book is meant to indicate that they did or did not assist me.) Those who did help me, however, certainly know what I owe them. And I *can* thank, by name:

Ruth, who had the idea; a different Ruth, Ruth Marcus, who helped me out; Ken Goldstein, who egged me on; Jeannette Kossuth, who saved my life; and my parents, who made this and everything else I've done possible;

Ellis Henican of *Newsday*, whose column suggesting that books be written about intriguing city departments other than the Police Department inspired me in the last stages of writing this book;

The reporters who were fearless, enterprising, and persistent enough to tell parts of the DOI story to the public: Janet Allon, Sean Assael, Wayne Barrett, Andrea Bernstein, Joe Calderone, Dominick Carter, Mary Civiello, David Firestone, Kevin Flynn, Gail Collins, Terry Golway, Ellis Henican, Dennis Hevesi, Dan Janison, Andrew Kirtzman, Andy Logan, Marcia Kramer, Lucette Lagnado, Rosemary Lavan, M. P. McQueen, Michael Moss, Jack Newfield, Joe Queen, Selwyn Raab, Barbara Ross, Rosanna Scotto, David Seifman, Joel Siegel, Mary Gay Taylor, Mike Weber, and others;

The Houston gang, who let me know how they do it out West and whose stories are incorporated in this book, including my sister, Wendy Benjaminson Hoagland, former political editor of the *Houston Chronicle, Chronicle* reporters R. A. Dyer and Julie Mason, and Jim Schutze, a former reporter for the *Detroit Free Press*, now serving as Dallas bureau chief of the *Chronicle*;

The inspector general of Chicago, Alexander Vroustouris, and his deputy inspector general, John A. Gasiorowski, for their assistance;

Lyle, Carole, and Sandra Stuart, for their skill and faith. As a boy, I always admired Lyle for his style and former Supreme Florence Ballard for her voluptuousness. When I grew up, I met them both. God take me now.

My brother Eric for his confidence;

My uncle, Daniel Galinson, for his continued understanding and free legal advice;

My new friends at my new job, Frank, Ed, Jim, and Mike Prial, Andrea Della Monica, David Garrick, Rayna Katz, Seth Kaufman, Todd Maisel, Harry Park, Tom Ponzo, Max Scotland, and Richard Steier;

Susan Cook, Nancy Dorvil, Ronald Schwartz, Pamela Stultz, Jennifer Zalatoris, and the Peter Harrigan family for their patience and understanding;

Some of my oldest friends: Thomas Adcock, John Brigham, Richard and Barbara Gervais Street Hagerty, Louis Heldman, David and Jeannie Horwatt, Ruth and Bernie Miller, and John Oppedahl for their continued friendship;

My favorite reporter, Susan Harrigan, to whom I'm married; our daughter, Anne, my favorite student, gymnast, and equestrian; and our totally undisciplined Yorkie, Scarlett.

TABLE OF
CONTENTS

9

THE RAID

*The time to guard against
corruption and tyranny is before
they shall have gotten hold of us.
It is better to keep the wolf out
of the fold than to trust on drawing
his teeth and talons after he shall
have entered.—Thomas Jefferson*

THE VAN SPED at sixty miles per hour up the FDR Drive toward
the Bronx. It was followed closely by another van. The scruffily
dressed men in the first van kept in touch by hand-held radio with
the even scruffier men in the second. It was 6 A.M.

Both vans were high-powered, late-model, and fashionable.
This made sense, since they'd both been confiscated from high-
powered, late-model, fashionable dope dealers.

Traffic was light. The vans made rapid progress. After a
jouncing, ten-second drive across the Willis Avenue Bridge, which
connects Manhattan and the Bronx, it wasn't long before they
reached their destination, a middle-class housing project.

One of the men, a balding pale-skinned man in his thirties, with a small pot belly and a thick Brooklyn accent, jumped out of the van before it had come to a complete halt in front of one the project's apartment buildings. With a key he'd taken from the super the day before, he opened the front door of the nearest building and let the eight armed men who accompanied him into its lobby. They raced up the stairs to the sixth floor and drew their guns. While several of the men covered the adjacent hallways and apartments, the Brooklyn man, followed closely by a heavy muscular man with darker skin, pounded on the door of one of the apartments with the butt of his heavy revolver. "Open up!" he said. "Police!"

He was lying.

A thin Latino man, who had obviously been roused from sleep, answered the door. He was wearing only cheap pajama bottoms. "You're under arrest," said the Brooklyn man and pushed his way into the apartment. A woman and a teenage girl, both wearing nightgowns, appeared from an adjacent room as several of the other armed men poured in. Some remained with guns drawn outside the apartment and at the end of the hallway in case the target's friends or neighbors decided to take it upon themselves to interfere.

As soon as she realized what was happening, the teenage girl began to scream, "You're treating my father like a criminal! You're treating my father like a criminal!" at the top of her lungs over and over again.

We *were* treating her father like a criminal, and with immense justification. He'd been part of a loosely organized group that had stolen at least $45 million from the city.

Some of the men on this raid were detectives on temporary assignment from the Police Department, but the others were civilian investigators, and all were under the command not of the Police Department, but of New York City's Department of Investigation (DOI), which, with a $20-million annual budget and 350 employees, was charged with investigating and arresting corrupt contractors doing business with the city and corrupt city employees and officials.

Although DOI arrests hundreds of people every year, it would have made little sense for the Brooklyn man—a DOI investigator—to shout "DOI!" while he pounded on the door. No one would have known what he was talking about. We were the city's secret police. (DOI agents often work undercover, they wear no uniforms, and they're only occasionally mentioned in the newspapers.)

And from 1990 to 1994, for the first and only time in our history, we, the secret police, were free from almost all the political restraints that had previously encumbered us. This is the story of DOI's investigations during those four years of freedom.

I was the executive assistant to the commissioner of DOI for two and a half of those years (mid-1991 to 1994). I held the same post during the first seven months of the Giuliani administration. Now that I no longer work for the department, I'm going to tell you all I can about my turbulent years with the city's secret police during our most active era ever, the cases we investigated, and the enemies we took on . . . and the department's subsequent rapid decline under the city's present mayor, Rudolph W. Giuliani. Some of what I'm about to relate you know about. Some you don't.

CHAPTER 2

THE TIME BEFORE

As long as I count the votes,
what are you going to do about it?
—*Boss Tweed, 1871*

New York City's immensely corrupt history gave rise to DOI.

The city had been victimized by corrupt politicians and contractors prior to 1873, of course, but the lid wasn't blown off the always-smoldering cauldron of civic corruption until that year, when the activities of political boss William Marcy Tweed and his ring were exposed. The Tweed Ring looted millions of dollars from a city much smaller and much poorer than today's megametropolis.

Tweed made two big mistakes, though. One, of course, was getting caught. The other was the Tweed Courthouse, also known as the "Palace of Plunder," which still stands just north of City Hall. Its cost had been estimated at $250,000. By the time it opened, it had cost twelve million (1872) dollars. One of Tweed's corrupt associates paid $125,000 to a carpenter to do one day's work on the courthouse. It can only be assumed that 99 percent of the $125,000 went directly into Tweed's pocket, which was his usual way of doing business.

The courthouse was a shoddy wreck within months and remains so today, in spite of numerous attempts to rehabilitate it. Most of the money appropriated for it had gone you-know-where. Very little had been spent on actual construction. The shock engendered by this monument to corruption, blighting by propinquity the elegant and austere City Hall building, which remains grand to this day, was too much for even the jaded to tolerate.

DOI was founded the year the Tweed Courthouse was completed—1873—to fight the corruption that courthouse symbolized.

First called the Commissioners of Accounts, the department, led by two commissioners, was charged with reviewing the expenditures of the city chamberlain and the city comptroller every three months, to be sure these officials were not robbing the city coffers. Gradually, but inevitably, as the city grew more and more complex, the Commissioners of Accounts assumed additional responsibilities, such as auditing the expenditures of other city agencies.

After three more reorganizations and expansions, the last in 1978, DOI assumed its medieval form.

Yes, medieval. Although by 1978 interplanetary probes were commonplace, Communism was on its last legs, and personal computers were on the way to millions of homes, DOI's investigators, metaphorically at least, staggered around in constricting suits of armor and found themselves forced to use crossbows against more realistically armed opponents.

The big problem was that most of the work DOI began doing later was then done by inspectors general, not by DOI. These IGs were employed by the same departments in which they were supposed to be catching crooks, including the crooks that might be their bosses. (Officially, IGs were required to report on criminal and other significant matters they uncovered to both their agency head and the DOI commissioner.)

All praise and blame accruing to the IG at, say, the Department of Transportation came from the commissioner of Transportation. If the IG for the Transportation Department wanted to get a raise someday, or, to get right down to it, if he wanted to keep his job, he had to be sure to a) not embarrass the boss and b) not arrest the boss.

Everything was okay if the IG arrested low-level crooks or mid-level crooks left in place by a previous administration. But if he happened to come across a mid-level or high-level crook appointed by his present boss, the transportation commissioner, his instinct would be to get the crook quietly out of the department without embarrassing the commissioner or simply leave the crook in place. Of course, should the crook be the commissioner, only the latter was a realistic alternative.

A case involving the Parking Violations Bureau, Queens Borough President Donald Manes, and Bronx political boss Stanley Friedman in 1987—in which DOI was only peripherally involved—changed all that. Mayor Edward Koch, who some said was ultimately responsible for the scandal, saw the PVB nightmare loom menacingly over his chances for a third term as mayor.

Whatever can be said against Koch, no one can ever say that he failed to speak and act energetically. And in his fight to control the damage done by the PVB scandal, Koch took an energetic and precedent-setting step. He issued Executive Order 105. This order, an attempt to show how much Koch hated corruption, removed the IGs from the control of the commissioners whose departments they were supposed to be investigating and made them employees of DOI.

From then on the field was reversed for the IGs. Now their promotions, their positions, their pay, their job security, and their self-respect were no longer the result of how well they got along with the people they were supposed to be investigating, but how well they did their jobs in the eyes of the commissioner of investigation—the head of DOI. Watershed events occurred. Some IGs left. Some transferred elsewhere. Some were let go, and some, frustrated under the previous arrangement, enthusiastically signed on with the new DOI.

For a while, though, it didn't matter. Koch liked to look good, but he had too much to hide to let the new system proceed unencumbered. So he did what Mayor Rudolph W. Giuliani would do some six years later. He appointed two of his pals in sequence to be DOI commissioner. His first, Kenneth Conboy, was a social friend of the mayor and was serving on Koch's staff when Koch tapped him for the top investigation slot.

But at least Conboy had experience as a prosecutor. The mayor's second DOI appointee, Kevin Frawley, had little law enforcement experience. His best credential, apparently, was having worked for Koch on his 1982 and 1985 campaigns. So, due to Executive Order 105, DOI might work more efficiently, but anything really damaging it found could be covered up by one or the other of the mayor's pals.

Koch, however, was swept from office in 1989, defeated by David N. Dinkins in the Democratic primary largely as a result of the PVB scandal. And Dinkins, of course, went on to edge out Rudy Giuliani, who was making his first try at the mayoralty.

Meanwhile, Executive Order 105 not only remained in place but was joined by a new city charter. Under the previous charter, the mayor could dismiss the DOI commissioner with a wave of his hand, along with any of his other commissioners. Under the new charter, which Dinkins supported, a strengthened and expanded City Council, headed by a powerful speaker, Peter F. Vallone, was given the power to approve or disapprove the mayor's choice of DOI commissioner. This made the council a full partner in that commissioner's appointment and ensured that the unilateral dismissal of the DOI commissioner by the mayor would be politically difficult in the extreme. The new charter also required that any mayor with the temerity to dismiss the city's chief investigator explain his reasons for doing so in writing and offer the dismissed commissioner an opportunity to deliver a public rebuttal.

All the machinery was in place. How well it would work depended on Dinkins's choice for commissioner of investigation. If he chose a pal, none of the charter provisions or the executive order would mean much. But Dinkins was either so honest or so naive that he not only appointed the first woman to run the Department of Investigation, but a woman who was so far from being his pal that she had never met him prior to interviewing for the job and had no ties to him, political or otherwise.* Not only that, Susan E. Shepard was a high-minded nonpolitical former federal prosecutor who had worked with DOI previously and who understood the department and its problems. She had no agenda, other than nailing as many bad guys as possible.

DOI's heyday had begun.

---

*Later in his administration, Dinkins cut DOI's budget more than he cut the budgets of other departments. Perhaps he was having second thoughts.

I'M HIRED

When I was a lad, I served a term,
As office boy in an Attorney's firm.
I cleaned the windows and I swept the floors
And I polished up the handle on the big front door.
I polished up the handle so carefully,
that now I am the ruler of the Queen's Navy.
—Gilbert and Sullivan, HMS Pinafore

It was the summer of 1991, and I didn't have a rabbi. You know, some kind of sponsor or bigwig who could get me a job in city government. Not as a typist, mind you, but as a high muckety-muck, with an office, a secretary, and a fat salary. Hey—don't get me wrong. I wanted to work, and work hard. But here I was rabbi-less, and what I needed was a decent government job.

Although I didn't have a rabbi, I did have John Kennedy's dog. I also had Fred Jerome, a friend who knew I was looking for a job. So one night, Fred's out walking and here comes his neighbor, Kennedy, walking his dog. Kennedy, who works at the Department of Investigation, tells Fred they're looking for a flack, or, as civil service jargon would have it in this instance, an executive assistant to the commissioner of investigation. Nice people, nice office, $70,000. Maybe not much to you plutocrats out there, but it sounded good to me. I send in my resume, go through a series of unremarkable interviews, and get the job.

I had read newspaper articles that implied, or said, that the Department of Investigation was the mayor's tool for covering up scandal or pretending to investigate it. And many of his appointees in other departments certainly had worked in his campaign and would be loyal to him. So why didn't the mayor offer the job to one of them? Or to a person suggested by a big campaign contributor?

This question keeps me tossing and turning a couple of nights until I realize, from the evidence of my own appointment and some other signs, what the change has been—they're gonna run it straight this time. The mayor's appointee as commissioner of investigation is actually independent, I decided, and she, the commissioner, not city hall, is appointing her own people without political advice or interference.

Just before I'm hired, however, I begin to get an inkling of the mass of corruption I'm up against. I learn, for instance, that Kennedy was reduced to asking his fellow pedestrians if they knew anybody who wanted the position because the guy they'd been all set to hire before me, who had gone through the extensive resume and interview process, had been fouled up by the background investigation. DOI had checked to see if he had any tax problems with state or federal agencies that might reflect on his character and/or be embarrassing to the department if they were discovered after he had joined up. Turned out the guy hadn't paid any taxes for years. Just didn't file. So they had to tell him they couldn't hire him. (Throughout my years at the agency, I was to keep hearing about such people, people who just wouldn't pay their taxes, ever. One of them was a major official in a major city agency. He hadn't paid his taxes for years, but nothing seemed to happen to him. In fact, he's still on the job.)

So I get the salary, the office, and the secretary, but I begin to think I'm in for something more: a scary ride in a clean car through the muck and squalor of big-city corruption.

OUR HEAVIEST WEAPON

The price of justice is eternal publicity.
—*Arnold Bennett*

There's a joke that circulates in law enforcement circles about three dogs from three different government agencies patrolling the airport at a baggage-arrival area. One dog is from the Bureau of Alcohol, Tobacco and Firearms, the second is from the Drug Enforcement Administration, and the third is from the FBI.

A suitcase comes down the chute, and the ATF dog stiffens and points. The agents open the case and find illegal guns and ammunition inside. "Hooray for the ATF dog!" everyone says. A little while later, another suitcase slides down the chute, and the DEA dog stiffens and points. Agents open the case and find cocaine inside. "Hooray, hooray for the DEA dog!" everyone shouts. Then the FBI dog runs over and sodomizes the DEA dog. "Hooray, hooray, hooray for the wonderful FBI dog!!" everyone shouts.

That joke may say more about the FBI than about anything else, but it also illustrates the attitude toward publicity of government agencies on every level. It's not what you do that counts, it's how many cheers you get for doing it.

City bigwigs claimed to be indifferent to publicity, as opposed to arresting criminals and cleaning up institutions, but sometimes I thought that publicity was all they were thinking about.

Sometimes thoughts became action. Joe DePlasco, the spokesman for the Department of Transportation, heard that a TV station was planning to tape some con men who were selling phony DOT documents to buyers right outside a DOT facility. The con artistry hadn't moved the department to action, but the threat of publicity certainly did.

Since publicity was DePlasco's game, he decided to handle the situation himself. He rounded up some DOT police, roared over to the scene, and arrested the men, leaving the TV people with nothing to film. Someone suggested later that this was as if the U.S. president's press secretary, hearing that a TV network was planning to tape a scene of carnage in an area U.S. troops were supposedly pacifying, gathered together some White House security troopers, flew them to the scene of the action, killed or drove away the malefactors, and then watched exultantly as the network news helicopter found nothing to tape.

It's no wonder that DePlasco, a master in his field, acted on a grand scale. At DOT, he was king. DOT Commissioner Lou Riccio told everyone on his staff if DePlasco calls, get rid of whomever you're on the line with, even if it's the president of the United States, and talk to DePlasco. I wonder how much importance publicity held in that department.

Publicitywise and in other ways, DOI, the agency I worked for, was surrounded by enemies. Most agencies tried to upstage us. Every other law enforcement or prosecutorial agency in the area was constantly trying to steal the limelight, when as far as I was concerned, 100 percent of the limelight was what we deserved 100 percent of the time.

Manhattan District Attorney Robert A. Morgenthau, although hardly the worst offender in this regard, was probably the most successful. We'd investigate a case, arrest the perps, and bring the case to Morgenthau's office. He'd then call a big press conference and talk about it as if it were his case.

Investigative agencies like DOI have to hand their cases over to prosecutors to get them prosecuted. However, Morgenthau's tactic made it appear as if he had investigated the whole thing himself and was now presenting his findings to a grateful public. He would credit DOI at these press conferences, but the reporters, having been invited over to Morgenthau's office for the conference, being handed releases with Morgenthau's name on top, looking at plaques representing awards to Morgenthau hanging on the wall, and watching Morgenthau's familiar lined and jowly face jawing away, could hardly avoid starting their stories with "X has been arrested and will be prosecuted for Y, D. A. Morgenthau announced today," leaving various DOI officials, especially me, virtually incoherent with rage.

Susan Shepard was totally against any publicity at first, but eventually she saw that getting credit in the media was a terrific morale builder for DOI staffers and helped preserve DOI and its independence. After all, the other departments had their own natural constituencies, while we had to create ours. If the Sanitation Department stopped picking up the garbage, you'd hear about it pretty soon. But without publicity, who would know what an undercover force like DOI was doing? So Shepard, under intense pressure from the rest of us, began counterattacking the publicity hounds at other agencies in a number of ways, all of which, I'm sure, pissed off Morgenthau and others no end. Nevertheless, she dragged her feet even while we tried to drag her into the spotlight. For some reason, she seemed to think that catching criminals was more important than getting credit for catching them.

Sometimes she would invite reporters and photographers over to her office to talk about a case, pick up a few good quotes from her, and get it set in their minds that this was a DOI case. Then we'd all be limou'ed over to Morgenthau's press conference, the reporters among us presumably inoculated against Morgenthauism. Or she would be sure to deliver the longest and most interesting statement at the Morgenthau press conference, complete with exquisitely tapeable props, such as tampered-with parking meters, in an attempt to dominate the image forming in the minds of the reporters.

Sometimes we'd attempt to steal the show by announcing the press conference to AP and UPI in DOI's name and mentioning Morgenthau's office merely as the location of the event. Once we scored a big coup with the TV stations by bringing to the conference tapes of perpetrators in similar cases performing their crimes, as recorded by a hidden camera, and printing "Department of Investigation" on the tape itself. The tape was a natural for broadcast. How often do you see a picture of a real perp committing a real crime? It was the footage used in all the TV newscasts of the story.

Our most successful tactic, though, involved scoops of one sort or another. Sometimes we'd invite a reporter and photographer from one, and only one, newspaper to go along with us on a raid. The raids were usually held around dawn, so the reporter and photographer would rush back to their office after the raid, write their story, print their exclusive photographs, and have it ready to turn in by the time Morgy or some other interloper would hold his press conference later that day. If the reporter bothered to attend the press conference at all, he'd do it to check what he already knew and pick up any extra detail that might be lying around more than anything else. But he'd already have his story—and he'd have it early—making him his editor's darling twice over.

Shepard found journalist-accompanied raids distasteful, and other law enforcement agencies may have been jealous of our success with these tactics, or considered them showboating, but I saw them as unvarnished truth-telling. Why let anything stand between the reporter and his story? In any case, we had no choice. It was self-defense.

Best of all was when we could influence the reporter involved to skip Morgenthau's press conference altogether. One particular reporter, tormented by deadline-fixated editors, loved it when Shepard and I invited him over and told him about the whole case early on the morning it broke. He'd then write the story, turn it in before Morgenthau's press conference started, usually in the afternoon, and never bother to go to Morgy's press conference at all. One for us, none for Morgy.

Agency rivalry, constituency-building, and truth-telling aside, there was a special reason why PR was so important at DOI. In many cases, the people we arrested weren't planning to stay with the city anyway, so losing their pension eligibility wasn't a problem. Since they often had no previous record, it was a rare judge who would send them to jail for any length of time or, in many cases, at all. So that left the press release as the only punishment, one that might indeed have a deterrent effect on their careers as well as warn others away from them. On many days I felt like the Lord High Executioner, waving my sharp-edged press releases on high.

CHAPTER 5

TWIN TOWER TERROR

Rank corruption, mining all within,
Infects unseen.—Shakespeare, Hamlet

People have a way of projecting their anger over their helplessness onto those who rescue them from it. Never did this become more obvious than when DOI found itself enmeshed in the World Trade Center bombing.

I felt particularly involved in this case because DOI became entangled in the Trade Center explosion as a result of a fellow public information officer feeling powerless. Harry Ryttenberg, then employed as the Fire Department's flack, felt himself helpless to defend his agency from the ugly rumors directed at it after the explosion.

It was no wonder Harry felt bad about being unable to defend the Fire Department. An assignment editor for a local TV station before he was hired by the FDNY, Harry was a fire enthusiast who listened to calls on the citizens band radio and showed up at fire scenes on his own time.

I myself, although not a fire freak, always suffered personal pain when federal prosecutors and the Manhattan district attorney got credit in the papers for DOI's cases. So I was able to sympathize with what Harry must have felt when he signed on with the Fire Department, only to discover within a short while that rumors were being repeated everywhere about the allegedly slimy conduct of the firefighters he believed to have been heroically involved in the Twin Towers disaster.

Harry thought he knew who was spreading the rumors: the Port Authority police, one of the city's uniformed forces that competed with the Fire Department for publicity. The Twin Towers were Port Authority facilities, and the PA cops had been the first to respond to the blast. After all, they were right on the scene.

But, in a world where media credit is almost everything, and real accomplishment almost nothing, they hadn't received the media credit they thought they deserved. And it's just possible that they initiated, or at least spread, the rumors about those who had received most of the attention: the firefighters.

It's also possible the New York Police Department began or circulated the rumors. The rather juvenile contest between New York's "Finest" and its "Bravest" was well into its second century by the time of the Trade Center explosion and showed no signs of abating. No verbal holds were barred. I once asked a high police official why he hadn't become a firefighter. "I failed the firefighter civil service test," he replied. "I couldn't get down the stairs with a TV set in my boot." Sometimes physical holds were used. On at least two occasions in the past few years, police officers have arrested firefighters who allegedly "got in their way" at crime/fire scenes.

The Twin Towers rumors came in many shapes and colors. Some were serious. Firefighters responding to the Trade Center bombing had broken into the Port Authority Credit Union office and the Citibank branch in the Trade Center and had stolen an undisclosed amount of cash. They had tampered with crime-scene evidence. They had broken into unoccupied offices and had stolen typewriters, computers, and other items from them. They had broken into autos parked in the explosion area.

Some rumors were silly. Could anyone actually believe that firefighters had walked off with an automatic teller machine? Or that they had lifted $2-million-worth of tools and machinery from Storage Level B-1? They had bothered stealing a box of chocolates from a candy store in the Trade Center concourse? They had tried to break into telephone coin boxes with hatchets? They had removed an x-ray machine and a computer from the trunk of the presidential limousine kept in one of the Trade Center garages? They had stolen $150,000 in cash, etc.? Harry, in an emotional memo to Commissioner Shepard, demanded that DOI root out and discipline whomever was spreading these rumors.

Shepard had better things to do with her investigators than send them out to arrest people for rumormongering. But she argued that DOI, charged as it was with investigating and arresting crooked city employees, including firefighters, could not sit idly by while such rumors circulated. Dissenters in the department pointed out that most DOI cases started with a complaint or a tip about wrongdoing or were the result of a DOI auditor or investigator coming across evidence of criminality. They argued that what Shepard proposed was starting an investigation based on rumors of complaints rather than on the complaints themselves.

The dissenters were unable to convince Shepard, and a major part of the task was checking out the rumors to see if a crime had been committed. This assignment was given to Lieutenant Ed Norris, the commander of the DOI Squad, the thirty or so cops assigned to DOI duty. (DOI investigations and arrests were often carried out by mixed teams of squad members and DOI special investigators. Special investigators carried weapons and were peace officers. Confidential investigators didn't and weren't.)

Norris was a P. R. man's dream: his movie-star good looks made him wildly popular with women. But he took his work seriously, albeit in a theatrical way. His spacious DOI office featured his collection of police helmets from around the world. It also featured a *New York Newsday* photo of him lifting the blanket off a corpse that was lying in the middle of the street. He had a special fondness for that picture. Perhaps it reminded him of one of his early police assignments, patrolling Times Square on foot at night. It may also have reminded him, by way of contrast, of his second post, in a silk-stocking precinct on Manhattan's Upper East Side. If regulations had allowed it, he once remarked, during his years on the Upper East Side, he would have left his service revolver in the precinct house and carried a knife and fork in his belt, because the only real action on his tours of duty in that area was eating the many dinners he was invited to.

Norris and his team began interviewing anyone who might know of firefighter misconduct during the aftermath of the bombing. They interviewed officials of every police and security force involved in the rescue and every one of the merchants in the giant World Trade Center concourse.

As Norris and the others traipsed from store to store, asking each and every store owner if he had been robbed and who he thought might have taken what he may or may not have lost, you could almost hear the rumor mills revving up again, like giant rotary presses just below the concourse floor. It was impossible to prevent the store owners from talking to each other about DOI's questions.

A second wave of rumors immediately built itself into an irresistible wave. The FBI was investigating large-scale theft by firefighters. Twelve firefighters were soon to be arrested for Trade Center crimes. A city employee had made a videotape of firefighters looting ATMs, but the tape had been sealed away by officials.

Since no one would confirm any of these rumors, they remained underground, except in the reporter-flack nexus at the heart of the media underworld. Reporter after reporter called me and other flacks with the latest version of what he had heard and begged me to tell him whether he'd be right in going ahead with the story or grossly embarrassed by doing so.

When the fog of rumor had lifted and DOI's investigation was finished, the true picture became evident. Nothing was missing from the automatic teller machines. Every penny had been accounted for. Nothing was missing from the Credit Union or Citibank. Nothing had been stolen from the cars in the sub-basement or anywhere else. No store owners had reported any significant property missing. No tools were missing. Signs of forced entry were found on the doors of various stores and the credit union, but since nothing was missing and the firefighters had been searching the building for trapped or injured people, all agreed that these were signs of that search. It was no wonder that Norris agreed with his civilian partner, Assistant Commissioner Martha Hochberger, when she recommended in writing to Shepard that "the case be closed as unsubstantiated."

Only one incident, which had been mentioned in the *New York Times* shortly after the explosion, had been confirmed. The day after the explosion, various officials had gained access to the "Hors D'Oeuvrey" section of the Windows on the World restaurant (also known as "Widows on the Void" to some of its depressed female staff members), which revolved at the top of the Trade Center.

There the officials had found 150 empty beer bottles, two nearly empty bottles of cognac, and other similar detritus on tables near the bar. Near the empty bottles, it was said, was a napkin on which "Thank you for your hospitality" had been written. Who signed it varied according to who was being interviewed, but among the initials some officials remember were "FDNY" and "NYPD."

Restaurant personnel had thrown the napkin away, so all Norris had to go on was the varied testimony about who had signed it. And, of course, even if Norris had had the napkin, he would have been hard-pressed to prove that anyone representing those departments had actually drunk the alcohol it referred to. Officials said the beer bottles may even have been left there by customers. It's also quite likely that had the restaurant staffers remained at their posts, they would have offered free refreshment to the firefighters who had clambered to the top of the World Trade Center carrying heavy equipment in order to rescue them.

But it may have been this little incident, as well as interforce jealousy, that sparked the fire-thievery rumors and upset Harry.

The "Bravest" and the "Finest" haven't been sniping at each other lately, but they will be soon again, if only to keep the tradition intact. The "Widows on the Void" closed, although it later reopened. As for Harry, a few press conferences later, with the new mayor, Rudy Giuliani, present, Harry collapsed from a heart attack. He now works as the flack for the somewhat less rumor-infested State Division of Housing and Community Renewal.

BICOASTAL BONANZA

"Never complain, never explain."
—The very much married Henry Ford II,
to a Highway Patrol Officer when stopped
on the California coastal road while escorting
a well-known model.

Do those California bank tellers smoke weed day and night?

It's 1992. A man in his midtwenties drives through Los Angeles, past boarded-up drugstores where Hollywood stars were allegedly discovered, past hot-dog stands shaped like rocket ships, past neon-lit strip parlors, in a vehicle bearing "Bed Stuy 1" vanity license plates. When he gets to the bank he was looking for, he tells the appropriate bank official he wants to open an account in the name of "Stacy Little, doing business as City Collector, USMREAP." The bank official learns that "USMREAP" stands for U.S. Mortgage Reduction Equity Acceleration Program, which, unknown to him, was a nonexistent entity. Nevertheless, he agrees to Little's request.

Then Little starts depositing checks in the account. The checks are all made out to the "City Collector" for amounts ranging from a few hundred to many thousands of dollars. All the checks are written by companies in New York City. Little's somewhat nervous waiting for the first few checks to go through. Won't it look suspicious to somebody that these New York City taxpayer checks are being deposited in a California bank?

Occasionally, the tellers do wonder about the New York origins of the checks or note the discrepancy between the name on the check and the name on the account. But hey, what's one minor discrepancy among so many major discrepancies in life?

After his initial nervousness subsides, Little starts withdrawing large amounts of money from the account, day and night, week after week. No problem.

A few months later, he opens another account at a different bank under the name "Stacy Little, doing business as the New York Department of Finance and Interest Savings for Home Mortgages." Again, he's nervous for a short while because this time his name is attached to an account linking him without a shred of authorization to the New York City Department of Finance, which actually collects the city's taxes. No one notices or cares.

Again he deposits numerous checks from New York City companies and withdraws hundreds of thousands of dollars from the account, much of it in cash. Weeks go by. No problem.

Then, just when everything looks rosy, he makes a mistake. He deposits a check made out to the Department of Finance from the Metromedia Company in New York City. The teller on duty notices some odd things about this check. It's dirty and creased, as if someone has been carrying it around in his wallet for a while. It's a few weeks old. And it's made out for $495,000. But hey, there's a lot of other things to do than worry about this shit. He approves it for deposit.

The next day Little drives up to the same teller and hands him a withdrawal slip for $400,000 in cash. He sits there expectantly waiting for the teller to shovel $400,000 in tens and twenties into the drive-in window drawer.

A small flare ignites deep in the recesses of the teller's brain. Maybe there's something amiss here, he thinks. He sighs—being a Californian, he hates conflict—and tells Little he'll have to come back for his money in a couple of days, after the check clears. Then he shows the check to the bank manager and tells him the story of the account.

The manager becomes alarmed and communicates his suspicions to a New York City Department of Finance official via telephone. That official also becomes alarmed. He's been getting calls from companies that have paid their taxes but have been unable to stop the flow of dunning notices and phone calls from the Finance Department. Other companies have called to say that the checks they sent in to pay their New York City taxes have been deposited in a California bank, which seemed peculiar.

The Finance official calls DOI, and Inspector General Vinnie Green starts reviewing procedures at the Finance Department to see who might have received such checks. Immediate suspicion, of a humorous sort, falls on Robbie the Robot, a mechanical being that trundles checks both large and small around Finance. Robbie saves the department some salary money, but he isn't much of a watchdog. His handler in each Finance unit is supposed to take the checks and mail for his department only from that department's slot in Robbie's chest. But anyone in any department, or anyone in the hall, for that matter, can take any check he likes from Robbie, and Robbie won't tell a soul. Robbie's a robot, not a stool pigeon.

Then, on a more serious note, one of the DOI investigators involved realizes that until a department employee logs in a check from a taxpayer, there's nothing to stop anyone from taking any checks he likes, except fear of an eventual protest way down the road from the taxpayer who sent it in. The DOI investigator also realizes that the dishonest official might think that if he set up a bank account that would make it appear to the taxpayer as if the check had been deposited in a Finance Department account, he could postpone a taxpayer complaint for quite some time.

Suspicion soon falls on Damon Sidberry, a $17,675-a-year Finance Department clerk whose job is to open much of the mail and log in many of the checks sent to the department. Soon it becomes clear that Sidberry's been sticking checks in his pocket as they come in and sending them to Little, a former Marine who served in the New York City area while in the corps. Sidberry has sent the jughead, who could barely live on his pay while a Marine, seventy-seven checks worth a total of $700,000.

Little, in turn, has used a lot of the tax money Sidberry has sent him to buy California real estate, a pickup truck, stereo equipment, a pool table, a townhouse, jewelry, and airline tickets. The whole arrangement might appear to be charity on Sidberry's part except that records show that on one occasion Little sent him $10,000 in cashier's checks. Even more incriminating for Sidberry, Little has never sent any other checks of any sort to any other Finance Department employee. Little is even more generous with his brother, Anthony. He sends him $34,000. And, unfortunately for all concerned, phone records link Sidberry and Anthony Little, both of whom live in Brooklyn while Stacy Little grooves away on the left coast.

While all this is going on, Anthony, possibly trying to change his way of life, applies for a job as a correction officer in the city's jails. The required physical examination shows cocaine in his system, and his application is rejected. So much for his attempt at honesty.

But DOI does more than reject him. It arrests him and Sidberry. Sidberry's charged with the federal crime of conspiring to steal and transport stolen taxpayer checks through interstate commerce. Anthony Little is charged with receiving proceeds from the stolen checks. Meanwhile, the FBI arrests Stacy Little in California on the same charge applied to Sidberry. Sidberry receives a three-month sentence and Stacy Little gets twenty-one months respectively behind bars.

The Finance Department promises it will reform its procedures. But, as Shepard remarks, it's very difficult in any city department to stop money coming in the front door from going out the back.

CHAPTER 7

RINGS WITHIN RINGS

Our sires' age was worse than our grandsires'.
We their sons are more worthless than they.
So in our turn we shall give the world a progeny
yet more corrupt. —Horace

It was the wigs and the makeup that really got me. The wigs and the makeup that the gang, which consisted almost entirely of females, used to steal $45 million from the city. Maybe it was the fact that the ringleader owned two Cadillacs. Or maybe it's that this was our chance to make a big score on the national scene— and a lousy perp blew that chance out of the water.

It all began when a very religious and very poor woman decided that she needed to go on welfare but was refused because she had too many assets to qualify.

Discouraged, the woman returned to her neighborhood and told a few friends what had happened. She soon was contacted by a friend of a friend who offered to open a welfare case for her for $2,000. The friend of a friend said she'd already done it for a great many people, told the discouraged woman how much each of those people was receiving, and said there was no need to fear detection. The clerks at the welfare center didn't care who got the money they gave away, the friend of a friend said.

There was no need to fear arrest, either. No one was watching. As it turned out, she was wrong. DOI was watching. But for various reasons, it won't ever be watching again.

The woman who had been turned down said no. She believed in God; she did not believe in dishonesty. And there the matter sat until she remembered that the woman who had phoned her had said that she was doing this for a lot of other people. Maybe she could eliminate a bit of the dishonesty that so troubled her in the world if she notified the authorities. So she did.

Her account of the conversation eventually reached Steven Pasichow, DOI's inspector general for the Human Resources Administration, the city's welfare department. What the thief didn't know was that Pasichow's staff was so large—supported as it was, in part, by federal welfare funds—that it took up an entire floor of the large downtown office building that housed the welfare agency. His unit was by far the largest concentration of DOI investigators in the city. But Pasichow and his subordinates patrolled a monetary dike that leaked from a thousand holes. They were continually investigating thefts of every description, but didn't bother to open files on cases where only small amounts were involved. If they had, they would have been so overwhelmed with petty cases, they would have achieved nothing. This case, though, sounded as if it was a group effort, and followed a pattern, which meant that once its secret was split open, it might turn out to be worth the time expended on it.

The honest welfare applicant had provided Pasichow with two essential pieces of information, which she recalled from her conversation with the welfare thief: the name of one welfare center where the scheme was active and the amount of money at least one of the phony welfare applicants was receiving.

Pasichow decided to check a random sample of the recipients who were receiving that exact amount of welfare at that center and immediately uncovered the investigator's equivalent of gold. A check of the social security numbers these recipients were using indicated that hundreds of the numbers, while resembling actual social security numbers, were not legitimate. The Social Security Administration hadn't issued them yet. There was something else unusual about many of these recipients—they lived together. In fact, twelve of the recipients and their two children each were listed as living in the same small apartment.

After a few more days of computer searching, Pasichow's investigators had identified 900 such welfare recipients with bogus social security numbers, who had applied at the same welfare center and who shared other characteristics as well. All of them were female, their husbands were absent, and they claimed two or more children of preschool age, including an unusually high incidence of twins. (As it turned out, they claimed that these nonexistent children were preschoolers so that welfare officials wouldn't be able to check with schools and find out the kids didn't exist.) When eligibility specialists at the welfare center had asked for birth certificates as part of the welfare application process, these applicants had presented Puerto Rican birth certificates for themselves and city birth certificates for their dependents.

They also cashed their welfare checks in neighborhoods far from those they allegedly lived in. (It was discovered that they had paid off check cashers in the other neighborhoods to cash checks made out to them under several different names.) In the vast flood of welfare paperwork—at the time, almost one million city residents were on the dole—this island of apparent illicitness stood out clearly on the computer printouts that filled Pasichow's office.

———

He decided to leave the safety of the computer screen and start checking the printed and photocopied records of the eighty-one most suspicious cases. Each of these records contained a color photograph of the applicant, and the first reaction was a tremendous letdown among his keyed-up investigators. All the applicants appeared to be different people. Pasichow was hugely disappointed. Apparently he had done all this work for nothing.

But he wasn't about to give up. So he laid out all eighty-one identification photos on a big table, and he and his investigators walked around and around it, scrutinizing the photos for the slightest indication that any of them were actually pictures of the same person.

Eventually, someone noticed that the woman with her black hair up looked very much like the woman with her red hair down and an entirely different makeup scheme. Thus began the great matching game. As the number of unmatched photos shrank, the game got easier and easier. Soon every photo had been matched with one, two, three or four others. A subsequent visit to the Bureau of Vital Records showed that the birth certificates these people had presented for themselves and their nonexistent children were fake.

You'd think this would be a lot of trouble to go through just to open a few phony welfare cases and collect the checks involved unless you knew that a family of four on welfare received about $618 each month in cash and $245 worth of food stamps. If all 900 cases were fraudulent, that meant these cases were costing the city $775,000 a month, or $9.3 million a year.

Some of these cases had been open—receiving public money—for as many as ten years. Conservative estimates, therefore, indi-

cated that Pasichow was looking at a theft of about $45 million
worth of welfare payments, far and away the largest such theft ever
discovered. Individual crooks could easily prosper with $45 mil-
lion to divide among them. In fact, several of the perps were well
off enough to live in the Dominican Republic and fly in for the peri-
odic visits they were required to make to the welfare center to say
with downcast faces that they still needed their monthly subsidies.

Now came the fun part: arresting the perps. Pasichow had a
big problem, though. Many, if not all, of the addresses on the
phony welfare applications were themselves phony. Obviously
some or all of the names were, too. It would have been standard
procedure to arrest each person, individually, at her home. But
arrest who, at what home? So a ruse was devised. A number of
the perps, under only one of their identities each, were ordered
to report to the welfare center for a special recertification. When
they showed, they were hauled away by DOI agents.

The fun had only begun. Many of those arrested were rela-
tive small fry who had opened only one or more cases in their
own names. But the scheme had been progressing for so long and
with such success that many of the more entrepreneurial spirits
involved had decided to vary their roles.

Some had become, in part, "address merchants," who sold
other phony welfare clients, for $50 a month, the right to use their
addresses as mail drops for letters from the welfare center. Others, who became too busy handling their own phony cases to open
up any more, sold packets of fake documents and tips on how to
create cases to prospective phony welfare clients.

Since some of the women who bought these packages of documents didn't have the cash to pay for them up-front, they were
allowed to take the documents in return for a percentage of each
welfare payment they received as soon as they opened a case.
Some, mimicking Wall Street mortgage bankers, sold off their interests in these portions of future welfare payments to investors who

gave them cash up-front. A market in welfare futures developed.

Some, higher up in the chain, made up packets of documents and sold them to the middlewomen who sold them to the prospective phony clients. At the top of the chain, two printers in Florida—the only men involved—counterfeited blank birth certificates, social security cards, and child immunization records that they shipped off to a woman in suburban New York for $78 a set. She spent her time at a PC in her suburban den entering onto the documents the phony names chosen by the perps and selling the personalized sets to middlewomen for $1,000 a set. The middlewomen sold them to friends and relatives and at welfare centers for $2,000 each. Only the amount of paperwork they felt they could handle limited the number of cases that could be opened by each perp. One opened twelve and collected more than $300,000. Let me say in defense of the perps that the work involved in this scheme was hardly minimal. Several resigned from factory jobs they held to work this scam full-time. Some perps took on more than one of these roles, and complicated triple-identity situations arose.

Pasichow's people discovered all this in large part by painstakingly interrogating those arrested and, in classic police fashion, working their way up the chain.

But a couple of big questions still troubled and intrigued the inspector general. The welfare clerks' computers were supposed to check each applicant's social security number and did. In fact, a flashing light on the console alerted the eligibility specialist involved if the number was no good. So why were cases opened after the light had flashed? Because the light was always flashing. Every little error set it off. If someone had written "St." on one form and "Street" on another, the light would go wild, so no one paid it any mind when it flashed for real errors.

The other big question in Pasichow's mind was how many government employees were knowingly involved. Not merely sloppy workers, but conspirators who allowed these cases onto the rolls, in return for bribes, year after year. As it turned out, there were some, but only some, and their only real function seemed to be to come to the rescue if anything went wrong, which it rarely did. The phony documents and disguises were so good and the system so porous that government workers were unnecessary. Private industry did the job.

And it did a profitable job. The city's pie is so gigantic that even a crumb from its edge can mean a lot of extra spending money for a few. The beneficiaries of the scheme bought jewelry and houses, went on dayslong gambling sprees, and rented the services of clowns for their children's birthday parties. Three of the perps, having gained so much experience with makeup and hairstyles, used their earnings to open up a beauty parlor.

While the arrests of the lower-downs were relatively routine, the arrests of the higher-ups were not. Some were arrested in other states by DOI agents grateful for the out-of-town trips. Some fled and were arrested at DOI's request by police in other states. Some were picked up at airports by customs agents who spotted the people from the DOI agents' descriptions.

One woman, in a scene that would have made Ronald Reagan's heart sing, was arrested while she was sitting in one of the two Cadillacs she and her husband owned. DOI cars pulled up in front and in back of her car and on its street side while an agent effectuated the arrest through the passenger door. (This couple owned two other cars as well and were also active in other areas of life. The woman had her seventh child, in jail, while awaiting her initial hearing in the welfare case.) Others were arrested at their homes in early-morning raids, including the fellow arrested in the raid with which this book begins.

One of the out-of-state arrests took place in Florida, a special treat for the usually city-bound DOI detectives. Those detectives chosen for the trip, however, were the targets of a very effective trick by those who remained behind. The lucky ones who went to Florida had identified themselves as detectives when they rented their rooms. They soon discovered that the extended family that owned the motel was made up of law-and-order enthusiasts. As far as the motel owners were concerned, nothing was too good for the cops who were honoring them by staying at their establishment. Food was brought up warm from the oven, huge suitcases were cheerfully carried, towels were changed twice daily, and cars were washed free of charge as surprise presents for the honored guests.

The jealous DOI cops stuck in their offices back in Manhattan heard about this and about the standard balmy Florida weather and decided they couldn't take it anymore. One of them called the motel when he knew the detectives would be out and asked if he could leave a message. The message was "Good boy-hunting." When asked to repeat himself, the cop said, yes, the message meant just what the clerk thought it meant, that both he and the cops at their motel were members of the North American Man-Boy Love Association, a real group that encourages man-boy love in spite of the various laws against it. He started to wax enthusiastic about the pleasures of man-boy love, but the clerk hung up on him. From then on at the motel, nothing was too bad for the visiting cops. Asked for room service, the staffers shot back, "We don't provide room service for your kind." Asked to provide receipts, the staffers refused. The cops spent the rest of the trip wondering what "your kind" meant. When they returned to DOI, they were gleefully told.

Practical joking aside, the arrests of the welfare thieves began what may have been an even-greater expenditure of government money than a year or so on welfare would have cost the government if the perps had been allowed to continue their fake claims. Since most of the women had legitimately filed their own welfare cases, they were, ipso facto, considered welfare cases and unable to pay for attorneys. That meant the government paid for private attorneys to defend them, a common alternative to assigning public defenders to handle cases. Tax-paid prosecutors were assigned to the cases, and assistant prosecutors, and secretaries, and researchers. A pack of highly paid taxpayer-financed spiders descended on the crooked flies trapped in DOI's web. Months of preliminary hearings and motions began, but DOI's case was so good that all the cases ended in plea bargains rather than trials.

The guilty pleas and the sentencings went on for months. Because of the more than one hundred defendants involved, the multilayered and somewhat bizarre nature of the scheme, the sentencings themselves—at one of them, the judge, noticing how many Dominicans were involved, urged the Dominican community to clean its own house, a remark that didn't go over too well in Dominican neighborhoods—we received a fairly sustained run of publicity.

It also brought us *Primetime Live* and an attempt at intervention from Lee Jones, the mayor's press secretary. *Primetime*, preparing a show on welfare fraud nationwide, could not help but be attracted to DOI's massive welfare-fraud case. *Primetime* star Diane Sawyer interviewed Shepard, one of the perps, and several DOI investigators over a period of weeks. Guessing what Lee Jones's reaction might be, Shepard and I somehow forgot to tell him about *Primetime*'s interest. He finally heard about it from the welfare department's press office when the show's reporters began asking them how the scandal had occurred.

Lee's reaction was predictable. He screamed at me on the phone about how OUTRAGEOUS and SLOPPY it had been for us not to let him or the welfare department know until just about the last moment and how we were trying to MAKE OURSELVES LOOK GOOD BY MAKING OTHER DEPARTMENTS LOOK BAD!!! I was tempted to tell him that you could hardly find a better definition of DOI's publicity mission than that, but, wisely, I held my tongue.

The perps won the biggest of the publicity battles, however. The raid on that Brooklyn apartment I described in the first chapter was filmed by a *Primetime* TV crew. The screaming teenager, the half-clothed perp, the nightgowned wife, the fully dressed, all male DOI investigators with heavy service revolvers drawn, peering down the hallways of the building in case any neighbors decided on violent intervention—it all made great footage.

But a territorial dispute got in the way. The arrest had been made in the territory of the U. S. Attorney for the Southern District of New York, which had handled very few of the more than one hundred arrests involved. Southern District attorneys had not been involved in the case and had, therefore, not received any of the publicity. They felt that by being asked to handle this one lone case—which in all likelihood would receive no attention—they would be cleaning the gutter in the wake of the giant publicity parade staged by attorneys for the Eastern District of New York, who had prosecuted most of the cases. The attorneys from Southern insisted rather peevishly that if Eastern District was going to get the glory, it had to clean up after itself by making this arrest as well.

The case had to be transferred to the Eastern District, therefore, and the easiest way to do so was to drop the charges against the perp in the Southern District and refile them in the Eastern. Dropping the charges was easy, and the Eastern District attorneys were about to refile them when *Primetime*, virtually without warning, decided to run the show that week. Trailers immediately began airing on national TV showing DOI investigators pounding on the perp's door.

The ads surprised us—we had no idea we were going to be such a feature of the show. They certainly surprised the perp, who nevertheless recovered from his shock long enough to see his chance for a blocking maneuver. Sitting at home on bail watching himself about to be arrested on national TV, he telephoned *Primetime* and threatened to sue if the footage of his arrest was aired. Normally they would have ignored him, but, as he told them, the charges against him had been dropped! He was an innocent man!

A *Primetime* staffer called me in a panic. I tried to reassure her that the charges would soon be refiled, but she wasn't buying it. A suit might cost them millions, and they had plenty of other material. The show was aired, but DOI went unmentioned, to Lee Jones's delight, although not to mine. I felt like staying in bed for a few years, then maybe trying for a new start as a sump-pump repairman.

But that wasn't the worst of it. The sentencing began.

Gordon Mehler, the federal attorney who handled many of the prosecutions that arose from these arrests, demanded stringent sentences for the arrestees, who had blithely stolen millions they didn't need from a financially stretched city. After all, most of them had stolen hundreds of thousands of dollars each and in some cases had refused to cooperate, or only pretended to cooperate, when arrested. And not all of them were poor, homeless waifs, either. One had a doctor for a brother and a Mercedes-Benz engineer for a father and two employed ex-husbands during the period she looted the city's welfare treasury.

Unfortunately, from the prosecution's point of view, these thieves came to court dressed in their most motherly and attractive outfits and sobbed piteously while the judge, an aged fed, addressed them. They bowled him over. The judge had a 108-page memo in which he explained the sentences he was about to hand down to a large group of the defendants. In it he noted that one of the mothers he had considered sentencing to an actual jail term, "typical of the group, shook with fear at the possibility that prison would wrest her from her children. Her two older daughters, both teenagers, sat behind her. The family had come to court directly from the younger child's junior high school graduation, which took place on a beautiful June day.

"When the family arrived, the older sister and the graduate—still clad in a white robe and sporting a medal for her accomplishments in English classes—displayed the high spirits of two young, successful women looking forward to future accomplishments. The mother, by contrast, quailed at the prospect of having to leave these children without her guidance in a crime- and drug-ridden neighborhood. In tears, she expressed in plain terms the dark irony of her situation: the crime that was intended to help her family now threatened to destroy it. The young women, once aware of their mother's terror and sorrow, began to sob . . . "

I was in the courtroom and was tempted to shout out that one of the reasons her neighborhood was crime-ridden was because she lived in it. But I managed to control myself.

If he were to sentence them to prison, the judge went on, "given that overcrowding causes defendants to be sent to far-flung locations, any prison term imposed on these defendants would likely have to be served in a place where family visitation would be almost impossible. Defendants would be thrown in with drug 'mules' and habitual criminals of sharply different economic and cultural backgrounds from their own."

Some might argue that they should have thought about the possible consequences before they organized a smooth-running, multimillion-dollar thievery machine, but nothing any of the attorneys said along these lines convinced Judge Softy.

"Despite the fact that many of the defendants have lived with a number of men in an unmarried state," he went on, "these woman are not now promiscuous. They seem to have sought stable relationships. Most are middle-aged, conservative women, primarily housewives . . . " Giving them medals would be too severe a punishment, I found myself thinking.

The judge also ruled out major fines and restitution since most of the defendants "are without assets and are unlikely to ever earn more than a subsistence wage."

Some of the government employees who were peripherally involved in the scheme were sentenced to jail for as long as four years, along with a couple of the top schemers involved. But a more typical sentence was "Five years probation, the first six months of which shall be served in home detention. Defendant may leave only for work, shopping, care of the children, religious services and as permitted by Probation . . . A $50 assessment is imposed. Restitution of $110,831 [what she had stolen] is ordered [but] Probation shall arrange for restitution payments so as to permit sufficient income for the family.

"During the period of probation the defendant shall provide 36 hours a week of community service, up to a maximum of 1,000 hours, unless otherwise directed by Probation because it is unduly burdensome in a particular period. If the defendant is gainfully employed earning income for at least 36 hours per week, such employment shall count as community service. In addition, for every hour of such employment defendant is to receive a credit of $10 toward the bill for restitution . . . "

Whatever small amounts of restitution most of the defendants would pay would come out of their legitimate welfare checks. Many of the short terms of "imprisonment" imposed were to be served in community service centers, from which the defendants could be released for work and emergencies. Even these sentences would not have to be served, the judge ruled, if the defendant left the country. Of course, if a defendant did indeed leave the country, then found a way to return under another name (a minor problem), she could sidestep her sentence entirely.

The judge's slaps on the wrist may have saved a few families, immoral as the mothers of those families may have been, but those same sentences killed the chance of any other operation as involved as this one being launched for the next forty years or so. DOI would be willing to do it, but the prosecutors wouldn't be. This was key. DOI, like other police agencies, had to persuade prosecutorial agencies to take the cases the investigators had pulled together. And prosecutors didn't enjoy going into courtrooms armed for bear and coming out with ridiculously small pelts. The lesson learned by all involved—don't bother arresting any but the least sophisticated welfare cheats; it ain't worth it.

CHAPTER 8

WHITE LUNG, BLACK HEART

But who ever yet discovered,
in the anatomy of any corporation
...a heart?—Howel Walsh

Sometimes I thought I had it rough, what with everybody at DOI riding me to get their names in the papers or keep the details of their investigations out of the papers (or both). I could count on reporters either ignoring Shepard completely or trying to get an interview with her at exactly the same time.

Then, after a while, I began to believe it was DOI's investigators who really had it rough. Their salaries were low, their tasks often tedious, and the results of their work frequently unknown. The people they arrested certainly didn't appreciate what the investigators were doing, and the general public rarely knew about the thefts of public money or the injuries and deaths those investigators had prevented.

The people I really should have felt sorry for, though, were those who had been severely injured by the criminals DOI arrested. Among them were a number of poor souls who have ended their short lives by coughing their lungs out as a result of the activities of some evil people who ran "employment agencies."

These "agencies" preyed upon the growing need for asbestos removers. Industry needed more and more of them, but the work could be very dangerous to both workers and passers-by, so government was soon regulating it heavily. By the mid-1980s, workers who wanted jobs in the city's burgeoning asbestos-removal industry were required to take a two-week privately run asbestos-removal training course and then pass a test administered by the city's Environmental Protection Department.

Nobody was ever expelled from the course or failed the test, yet both were terribly important. They taught procedures that would save both the asbestos removers and passers-by from white lung and other fatal diseases and included the type of protective clothing the removers should wear. Graduates of the course were given asbestos-removal cards to carry. They were the only workers legally allowed to remove asbestos.

The cards were high-tech in the extreme, loaded with impossible-to-reproduce holograms and other twenty-first-century antiforgery technology. No unauthorized person should have been able to reproduce them, but that pious hope was dashed one morning when an inspector for the Environmental Protection Department went beyond the routine call of duty at an asbestos-removal site he was visiting. Not only did he closely examine each card he was shown, he wrote down the numbers on each card and later checked them against the numbers stored at Environmental Protection headquarters. Not a single number matched. It would have been impossible to ascertain that the cards were fake had the perps been able to use real license numbers: the forged cards were so well made, they WERE the real cards, except for the numbers they bore. Environmental Protection asked DOI to investigate.

DOI's inspector general for environmental protection, Bob Vinal, sent his investigators from one asbestos-removal site to another all over the city until they found more workers holding illegitimate cards.

The investigators soon noticed something linking all the holders of the phony cards. They were recent Polish immigrants, with immigration papers as counterfeit as their asbestos-removal licenses. Agents of the U.S. Immigration and Naturalization Service were called in and soon teams of heavy-set INS and DOI agents were grilling the illegal asbestos removers one by one in small dark rooms in obscure government buildings.

Judicious threats of imprisonment and forced repatriation were delivered through Polish-language interpreters to each illegitimate cardholder and results were achieved. Each and every worker spilled the name of his supplier.

The suppliers were, or course, the "employment agencies." They were clustered on one block in Greenpoint, Brooklyn, a neighborhood loaded with immigrant Poles. These businesses were indeed employment agencies in the sense that they supplied some legitimate jobs to some qualified workers, but most of their clients were laid-off employees of former socialist enterprises in newly non-Communist Poland. Recruited by the employment agents, the Polish workers were provided with forged immigration and asbestos-removal cards. They then paid their own airfare to this country in order to remove asbestos, for relatively high wages, but with no knowledge of protective procedures whatsoever.

Vinal sent a Polish-speaking undercover investigator to the employment agencies to buy a set of all available cards. After a sufficient number had been purchased, DOI, FBI, and INS agents raided four of the agencies and arrested a number of their owners and operators for selling the phony asbestos-removal licenses. As a result of the arrests, the perps faced up to five years in jail and $250,000 in fines each.

Although the arrests halted the asbestos-card racket, it's not at all clear how many Polish immigrants—tough, hard-working fellows desperate to make a few bucks to support their families in a struggling Eastern European economy—picked up a future case of lung cancer or white lung in the process of ripping out asbestos in hazardous ways, or how many city residents will find their health damaged in future years because asbestos was removed near them, often day after day, by workers who didn't know how to remove it safely.

White lung, known more accurately as mesothelioma, is caused only by unsafe contact with asbestos. It may not strike for twenty to forty years after such contact, but when it hits, it's ugly, fast, and fatal. It begins with a pain in the chest or abdomen that signals the growth of a tumor, which causes severe pain. The tumor involved may grow so large, and the victim so thin, that the tumor can be seen attempting to push through the flesh. The victim has immense trouble breathing, sitting, and talking. Taking three steps is a major achievement for a mesothelioma patient, but it leaves him or her exhausted, gasping, and burning with pain.

"You'd rather have lung cancer than have this," one expert said. This wish is often granted, since lung cancer is one of the other diseases brought on by unsafe contact with asbestos.

Some patients undergo major operations aimed at ending mesothelioma, but nothing can stop it. Some do well for awhile, then go down a steep slope real fast. The end usually comes within a year. Some patients, their minds still sharp, merely stop breathing and die. The spouses of others hear them gagging in the middle of the night, wake up, and find they're gone. Those who heard them gagging may be next. Some spouses and children of asbestos workers have developed the disease merely from exposure to the dusty work clothing.

Maybe an instinctive dread of this disease caused the only recorded reaction to the work of the hot-card manufacturers. An NYPD patrol car was driving through Greenpoint a few days after the arrests and noticed an mob of men outside one of the closed employment agencies. The men, who spoke only Polish, seemed intent on storming the agency and roughing up its occupants.

Neither police officer spoke Polish, but both understood body language. While one officer held the mob at bay and called for backup, the other entered the agency, where he found the owner in its small bathroom, hurriedly attempting to flush hundreds of plasticized phony cards down the toilet. The cop, who knew nothing of the arrests, took the man into protective custody and sent the cards rescued from the commode to DOI, where they were added to the growing pile of evidence against the perps.

Unfortunately, in many of the cases, what one attorney described as "extraneous circumstances" but would not describe further—none of them connected with DOI's method of arrest—resulted in no sentences for the perps.

Since Vinal could not peer into the future and see that no punishment would be meted out to those he had at least temporarily put out of business, and was encouraged by the arrest of the card producers, he decided to probe deeper into the Environmental Protection Department. He directed one of his undercover agents to approach an employee of the department and pose as an asbestos-removal contractor willing to pay for official information on an employee who was suing him.

DOI officials didn't believe that contractors buying copies of workers' background files from city employees was a major or even a minor problem. In fact, a contractor who actually needed the documents to respond to a suit by an employee could have subpoenaed them, even though the records were confidential under normal circumstances.

What DOI bigwigs did believe was that an employee arrested for one small offense or another might point out significant wrongdoing to save his own skin. Once you confront someone with the evidence that they've committed a crime, you can threaten them with criminal penalties, the loss of their city pension, and disgrace, then get across the message that you'll let them off with a light penalty if they give you information on the illicit activities of someone higher up in the organization. Sometimes this works. Sometimes it doesn't.

The DOI undercover agent's offer to purchase the asbestos-removal employee's papers was accepted. While the conversation leading up to the exchange of the papers was proceeding, however, an incident occurred that is the stuff of bad DOI dreams.

The underlying problem was that DOI maintains a large and varied fleet of cars confiscated from criminals. Not only do they cost the taxpayers nothing, they are readily accepted in the criminal environments DOI agents make every effort to penetrate. The investigators use these cars in undercover investigations, but they also park them in the city during the day and put DOI parking placards on the dashboards to avoid parking tickets.

When the DOI undercover went to buy the records from the corrupt employee, he consummated the deal in his DOI undercover car, parked in front of Environmental Protection headquarters. While the investigator was talking, the corrupt Environmental Protection employee saw something gleaming in the passenger-door side pocket and pulled out . . . a DOI parking placard.

"What are you doing with this, Mister Asbestos Contractor?" he asked.

Agency wags, quick thinking as always several days later in the air-conditioned safety of their downtown offices, proposed that the undercover should have said, when the placard was discovered, "Oh that? That isn't mine. I got it from another DOI undercover investigator."

The alternative suggested response, which I believe would have worked and might possibly have given this investigator the opportunity to make two cases in one: "You want one of those? I bought it for $50 from a guy who told me, and he was right, that you can park anywhere with it."

However, the actual investigator, remembering that he was still playing the role of sued asbestos contractor, actually said, "Yeah, see that? My lawyer wants me to find out about that guy, too." Few people could have thought faster on their feet and amazingly enough, the corrupt employee bought this quickly produced explanation. It was too bad for him, though. A few moments later, he took the money, and the agent arrested him.

Sad to say, this employee knew nothing of any other wrongdoing in his department. At least that's what he claimed. Perhaps he knew nothing more, or perhaps he feared the crooks above him in his own department more than he did the investigators from another.

WHEN DOCTORS GO BAD

I have said to corruption,
thou art my father; to the worm,
thou art my mother.—Job

What made DOI different from a lot of other police agencies, aside from its almost totally underground nature, was its concentration on white-collar criminals. Police Department detectives assigned to DOI expressed amazement at how clean, polite, well dressed, and well bathed most of our arrestees were. You could see them thinking: are you sure this is the perp?

I cheered them on when they made white-collar arrests. Violent street criminals are certainly the pits, but there's no reason to let thieves get away scot free just because they're relatively presentable. Even I, however, son of the middle class that I am, felt a slight touch of anxiety when we started arresting doctors.

The most interesting one we arrested was connected to a neighborhood—the South Bronx—that he undoubtedly imagined was far beneath him. The physician in question, Joseph Dubinsky, was paid by the city medical examiner to be on call eight hours a day to visit corpses who might have died from other than natural causes, in crime-ridden neighborhoods such as Mott Haven and Melrose.

The police didn't need a medical doctor to tell them that someone with a bullet hole in his head hadn't died a natural death. But there are subtler ways to kill someone, and the police weren't always able to determine if it was suspicious that one corpse had dilated pupils and another blotchy skin.

Dubinsky was qualified, not only to examine the corpses, but to interview roommates and relatives about the deceased's physical condition prior to death. By interviewing and examination, he could piece together the underlying reason for each death. The police would tell the relatives that the examining physician would be arriving soon to question them, and those relatives, while grieving, would wait for Dubinsky, who was considered a symbol of at least minimal municipal concern.

One day, however, after years on the job, Dubinsky decided he'd had enough. Of course, he could have resigned and allowed the city to hire a replacement. But over the decades, he'd grown greedy as well as lazy. So he decided the corpses of the South Bronx could fend for themselves, pretty much the same decision Mayor Rudy Giuliani made about the living residents of that portion of the borough only two years later.

Dubinsky also decided that while those corpses would now have to fend for themselves, he, Dr. Dubinsky, a respected and somewhat cosseted member of society, shouldn't have to. So he kept on filling out the paperwork as if he had examined the corpses. Rather than traipse around the Bronx, however, he'd call a cop at the scene and ask him for some details which he'd use to fill in the blanks. Meanwhile, he'd continue with his definitely less scummy work of examining private patients in his home office and charging high fees.

To give credence to the illusion he hoped to create—that he continued to care about the dead people only a few miles from his living room—he kept turning in mileage reports to the city and continued to accept the reimbursement for all the traveling he didn't do. At $168 a day plus 23 cents a mile, his virtually inactive municipal career continued to supplement his income quite nicely.

Like most of the other grifters, upper class or low, that DOI encountered, Dubinsky showed precious little fear of being caught. He was right not to worry about the disappointed bereaved of the mournful neighborhoods for which he was medically responsible. They complained, but who listened to them? But Dubinsky should have been smart enough to realize that grieving relatives weren't the only ones he was standing up. The cops also waited around for his appearances, until they became bored, and annoyed, and then gave up.

Some cops complained, and the complaints reached DOI. Appropriately enough, Shepard assigned a somewhat high-class pair of investigators, Phil Osattin and Karen Kramer, to look into the matter.

Osattin, a former therapist who had turned to investigation, and Kramer, an extremely intelligent attorney, one of whose daily thrills was taking a book out of the library and reading it cover to cover each evening, decided soon after interviewing enough disappointed death-scene participants that the complaints against Dubinsky were on the level.

Their solution to the case was elegant in its simplicity. They staked out Dubinsky's house for a few days while remaining in continuous two-way radio contact with various groups of cops who were busily requesting Dubinsky's presence at death scenes. When Dubinsky failed to show, but later turned in extensive paperwork indicating he had, the case was made.

DOI charged the doctor with the felonies of offering a false instrument for filing, falsifying business records, issuing a false certificate, and official misconduct. Since the defendant was a sixty-seven-year-old white physician felon, and not a fourteen-year-old black high-school dropout felon, he was sentenced to a mere $5,000 fine and 400 hours of community service in the Bronx. Perhaps his community service consisted of faking for free what he had been faking for pay previously.

Dubinsky's $5,000 fine and his community service effort couldn't do much for all those Bronx corpses who had been buried with little or no examination, however. In all likelihood, some of them had been murdered and declared dead of natural causes and their killers allowed to roam free, perhaps to kill again.

CLEAN STREETS MEAN MEAN HEARTS

If something stinks,
why stick your nose in it?
—Turkish saying

I loved it when we arrested inspectors. Most of them were white, making the arrests politically correct. And we usually arrested them in big groups, meaning we could use the daisy-chain technique. (We could use it, that is, if we could do it without Shepard knowing about it. To say the least, she considered this technique undignified.) What we'd do was notify the TV people we were going to have a perp walk behind the DOI building at a certain time. After booking the perps, we'd chain them together and load them into the back of a police van while the TV cameras rolled and guys with "DOI" prominently in view on their jackets guided them into the vehicle.

I'm not exaggerating when I say we arrested a lot of these people. Not only were there a lot of inspectors—sanitation, building, plumbing, health, electrical, restaurant, taxi, etc.—but a great many of them were corrupt. I can say this with some assurance because during Shepard's administration, we arrested half the city's taxi inspectors, half its plumbing inspectors, half its building inspectors, and a great many others.

We also arrested some sanitation police, who are essentially inspectors. Even I went into a daylong funk over this because . . . the city tries, it really tries. People complained over the years about the sidewalks being littered, partly by the merchants whose stores the sidewalks pass. The city responded by setting up the sanitation police, officially known as sanitation enforcement agents, men and women who drive around the city, issuing warnings and citations to merchants who fail to keep the sidewalks in front of their stores clean. The citations are a real threat. Fines escalate steeply for second and subsequent offenses.

Unfortunately, ten of these agents, hired to enforce cleanliness, became dirty themselves. Lacking adequate supervision, motivation, or training, they became, very early in the existence of the sanitation enforcement program, a roving pack of extortionists. They'd spend their days issuing just enough tickets to meet their guidelines and to make sure the local merchants remained continuously aware they retained the power to issue citations. They'd then spend the rest of each and every day picking up free clothing, free meals, and free cash payoffs. "I used my summons book like a gun, to get money," one of them said. Immigrants and street vendors were favorite targets, but no one was entirely safe.

DOI investigators who followed three of these agents for part of one day watched them pick up $75 in cash payoffs; free chicken and ziti for lunch; and one free "girl" each at a house of prostitution. Some agents picked up an extra, tax-free $10,000 a year this way in cash payoffs alone.

Although out of this amount they had to pay bribes to their supervisors to be assigned to the juiciest zones, sometimes they didn't need any assignments at all. One sanitation cop, who became known as "The Legend," continued to "work" even after he was dismissed from the force. He took his badge with him and continued for years to extort daily payoffs from merchants who didn't know he'd gone freelance.

But this group consisted of only 10 of the 130 or so sanitation cops. Many of the rest of them may actually have been honest. There was at least one exception, however, Marvin Henderson, whose arrest became the particular goal of Keith Schwam.

When I first saw Schwam, I tagged him as the most bureaucratic of men. Balding, pale, middle aged, and overweight, Schwam concentrated on detail. If this wasn't a city bureaucrat, who was? Yet he wasn't a clerk in the hall of records; he was a DOI inspector general, and, in theory at least, a hard-hitting Colombo. But his investigations seemed to take years. Years!

He also had a bad habit of bringing other agencies in on DOI investigations as joint investigators. This pissed me off no end, because it meant we had to share the credit when we broke a case, or even worse, hold the press conference on a big case at the headquarters of some other agency, making it extremely easy for every reporter present to forget about DOI when they took their notes and when they sat down at their terminals. I don't think that's why Schwam brought in the other agencies, though. I think he did because it gave him an excuse for taking as long as possible on every case and triple-checking every detail, since he had to coordinate endlessly with the other agencies he brought in and await their blessing for every step he took. But once Schwam made a case, it usually stayed made.

Schwam was even able to put the chains on Henderson. A sergeant in the sanitation police, Henderson spent part of his on-duty time working in one of the sanitation cops' field offices, where the summonses he and his subordinates gave out to merchants were processed before being sent on to the central office.

Henderson was conscientious about his job and interested in his work. As a good supervisor should, he often visited merchants his agents had ticketed earlier in the day to make sure they had received their copy of the ticket and couldn't claim later they never paid it because they never received it. He also stayed late at his job, after everyone else had gone home, to make sure all the paper-work was properly processed, even coming in Saturday evenings to move the flow along.

Indications were, however, that not was all as it should be with Henderson. His colleagues began to think that something was up and let DOI know. Sanitation was Schwam's area, and pretty soon he was plodding slowly along in pursuit of the wily Henderson.

Actually, he didn't start plodding immediately. He first spent seven days staring at the ceiling in his small, shabby office. His aides told visitors he was out of town. His mother worried because he didn't call. On the eighth day of his think-a-thon, he came up with a plan.

He obtained a key to the office in which Henderson worked. One early Saturday morning, when he could safely assume that no one would be present, including Henderson, Schwam and his crew entered Henderson's office and videotaped all the sum-monses Henderson's inspectors had issued the day before. Hen-derson, as usual, came in Saturday evening "to clean up."

On Monday morning, on Schwam's instructions, a Sanitation Department supervisor at the central office compared the tick-ets received there to the list DOI had prepared from the videotape. Some thirteen summonses, issued to twelve merchants, were missing. Henderson was stealing the summonses. But why?

To answer this question, the ever-resourceful Schwam arranged for an undercover operation within an undercover operation. A DOI investigator posed as a Fire Department inspector and "inspected," allegedly for fire code violations, the stores owned by the merchants whose tickets had been discovered missing. If the "inspector" discovered fire code violations at the store, he'd tell the merchant what he'd found and wait and see if the merchant offered him a bribe to overlook those violations. If so, according to the Schwam plan, the merchant would be arrested and then implicitly offered a lenient sentence if he agreed to reveal Henderson's scheme.

However, the one merchant who did offer a bribe, and was arrested for doing so, refused to cooperate. He probably knew he'd never go to jail for bribing one phony fire inspector. He also suspected that Henderson would make his life miserable for years afterward if he revealed the Sanitation sergeant's scheme to DOI.

So far, Schwam had made precious little progress. So he decided to install video cameras in Henderson's office to record the thefts of summonses as they occurred. But having done so, he ran into another problem. Henderson, for reasons unknown, suspected he was being videotaped.

Stop and think for a moment. What would you do if you were in Henderson's shoes? You strongly suspect a law enforcement agency taped you while you committed a crime. If you were to commit the crime again, another count would be added to the charges against you and another few months or years in a stinking, fetid, dangerously crowded jailhouse dormitory, full of lascivious cons who spend most their time pumping iron, would be added to your sentences. You'd stop, of course. I would. But neither one of us is Henderson. A drug abuser, Henderson needed the money his scheme was netting him. He needed the money nightly, he needed it continuously, and he needed it constantly. Stopping was not in his game plan.

Henderson was not totally irrational, however. He reasoned that DOI, to make a case against him for stealing the summonses, would have to incontrovertibly identify him on the tape. His solution: he'd enter the hallway outside his office dressed normally, but carrying an empty cardboard box. He'd then put the box over his head, enter the office that he suspected, correctly, was being videotaped, and steal the tickets. He'd then return to the hallway and remove the cardboard box from his head before leaving the building.

In a world as wildly irrational as city government, Henderson's scheme worked—the first time.

But Schwam, after a few hours thought, struck back at his target with a second more elaborate operation. At approximately 2:30 P.M. on a Sunday, while all the sanitation cops were out on patrol, Schwam and his investigators concealed themselves in positions from which they could tape the hallway as well as the office. Since Henderson's suspicions apparently extended only so far as his office door, this countermove succeeded. Schwam and company were able to tape Henderson donning his costume, entering the office, stealing the summonses, and removing the box in what he assumed was the safety of the hallway.

A few days later, the NYPD, in a move unconnected with Schwam's investigation, arrested Henderson, now known throughout the agency as "Boxhead Henderson," on a charge of possession of cocaine. Because the sergeant refused to undergo drug testing after being arrested, the Sanitation Department suspended him. But, like other city employees, Henderson seemed much more interested in his corrupt employment than in his legitimate work. Why should he allow an arrest and suspension to halt his illegitimate career? In any case, his need for drugs had hardly diminished during his night in the police holding cell.

A supervisor who returned to Henderson's office after hours a few days later to retrieve some personal belongings discovered Henderson once again pawing through the piles of summonses awaiting delivery to central. The supervisor knew Henderson shouldn't be removing summonses from an office where he no longer worked. He told him to leave, but the desperate sergeant wrestled the supervisor to the ground and fled with copies of several summonses. In his haste, however, he left the originals behind.

Schwam again sought the cooperation of the merchants to whom the summonses had been issued. This time a merchant agreed to cooperate, telling an assistant district attorney from the Manhattan DA's office, which Schwam had brought in on the case, that he had regularly been paying Henderson to dispose of summonses issued against his store by other sanitation cops.

Many other merchants had been paying Henderson for the same service. Since the payoffs were much less than the fines would have been, the merchants figured they were getting off easy. Henderson certainly was. He was paid his city salary for doing his job during the day and an unreported and untaxed private salary for undoing it at night. The only losers were, of course, the taxpayers—and the clean-sidewalk crowd.

Henderson got off easy. As far as the DOI case against him was concerned, he plea-bargained to one count of tampering with public records in the first degree and was sentenced to six months in jail. He may have spent less time in jail than it took to catch him.

CHAPTER 11

LIKE WATER THROUGH THEIR FINGERS

Of Ed Livingston, a man of splendid abilities,
but utterly corrupt. He shines and stinks
like rotten mackrel by moonlight.—John Randolph

Sometimes the forces arrayed against us were only a few blocks away, at City Hall; but in one case, that opposition emanated from the heavenly forests, fields, and mountains north of the city. It was there, far to the north of DOI headquarters, far from the teeming streets, where lay the pure lakes, bubbling streams, and quiet reservoirs from which the city drew its water, that we ran into our most implacable opposition and our biggest defeat.

As far from the city as this area is, it's the home of the city's water supply police. Founded around the turn of the last century, the water cops were organized when contractors hired by the city to build its upstate reservoirs and sluices, in their turn, employed thousands of immigrant workers to do the actual spade-and-shovel work. These foreign workers moved into a sparsely populated area where little or no law enforcement existed, frightening the region's farmers and merchants, who communicated their fear to the legislature. The legislature, in its turn, forced New York City to establish the water police and send the force upstate to protect the locals from the city's own workers.

There was some justice in all of this. The city of the time was big and rich and the upstate counties poor and small. The reservoirs were a city project, and there was no one else to do the policing job at the time. The state police were not formed until 1917.

Construction on the reservoir system continued for decades, and there was a case to be made for retaining the water police as a city force upstate during that time. During World War II, for instance, the water cops were charged with protecting the water supply from saboteurs and polluters as well as policing the workers. By the 1960s, the water system was finished, the workers gone—or integrated into local communities—the state police a powerful force, and a new city inspectional force, the watershed inspectors, had been organized and sent north to monitor the purity of the water supply.

In 1990, complaints about the water police caused Bob Vinal, DOI's inspector general for the Department of Environmental Protection, to order his deputy, Bob Frank, to begin an investigation of the force. It was discovered that no one had effectively communicated any of these post-1960 developments to the water police. Now firmly ensconced in their local communities, they ignored everything the city and its Department of Environmental Protection told them. They were able to get away with it partly

because the upstate communities wanted them there and continued to pressure the legislature to keep them there and partly
because city hall ignored their existence.

Frank and his investigators interviewed the water cops one
by one, in their cars, in their homes, and out on their back porches.
Even after talking to the cops, Frank found it difficult to say what
they did. They told him they went on patrol, but had no assigned
patrol routes, no sectors, no nothing. Each officer just took his
car out at the beginning of the day and went "on patrol," whenever and wherever he felt like.

Although the records of their patrolling were scanty to nonexistent, the records of their arrests painted a not-so-pretty picture
from the city's point of view. They spent most of their time setting up speed traps and arresting drunks in bars in the centers
of towns miles from the reservoirs.

They'd make these arrests at city taxpayer expense, then spend
hours in local courts processing the arrests and testifying about
them. The fines generated by their arrests, since they weren't collected in the city, went into the coffers of the towns in which the
arrests were made or into the state treasury.

In reality, the water police were working for the local towns
at city expense. But in their own minds, which were back in the
glory days of reservoir construction in 1900, they were still the
representatives, in what they saw as a poor rural area, of one of
the richer cities on earth. As ambassadors of a wealthy foreign
power in a benighted but strangely familiar countryside, the water
police felt justified in offering another freebie from the city treasury—firearms training for all local police departments within the
general area of the reservoir system.

But they had so much to do during the day as self-appointed
protectors of numerous communities of upstate residents that the
only way they could find time to fit in the firearms training was

on overtime pay (as the city fought frantically to cut its overtime bill by drastically limiting overtime for its downstate employees).

They also did much of their clerical work and training at overtime rates. Water police supervisors, some of whom lived ninety miles from their jobs, started every working day on overtime, beginning the moment they stepped into their cars to begin their drive to work. Since they were allowed to take their patrol cars home, they decided that they were working when they drove back and forth to work. The reasoning was they put in the required number of hours when they got to the job, so the commute was overtime.

Frank's major finding was that the water cops spent hardly any of their time doing what they were supposed to do: protecting the water system. They made virtually no arrests of people trespassing in or polluting the vast system which their responsibility was to safeguard.

The city responded by transferring the chief administrator of the water police to a job at Department of Environmental Protection headquarters, where, it was said, he raged constantly at the injustice done his former unit by DOI criticism of it. But Frank's report hadn't been all criticism of the water cops. He had pointed out that if the water police were actually to patrol the watershed, rather than the watering holes, their cars and radios were inadequate to the task. So the city bought them new cars and radios. Doing something else about them was discussed, but finally officialdom decided against it. Maybe the water cops could be used as a bargaining chip for something the city wanted from upstate residents some day.

THE WATER COPS MAKE THEIR MOVE

As I was going up the stair,
I met a man who wasn't there.
He wasn't there again today;
I wish, I wish he'd stay away.
—Hughes Mearns

To my great surprise, DOI, with its $20-million-annual budget, its 300 or so employees, its police powers, and its secretive nature, didn't go berserk . . . at least while I was there. The CIA and the FBI have, the Chicago and the Los Angeles Police Departments have, but not DOI. It was a shock to me, therefore, to see a related police agency, even an agency as weird as the water police, launch itself into insanity. Here's how we found out about it.

The replacement for the water police administrator who was kicked upstairs to the DEP, on taking over, went through the rather sparse files the water cops had maintained. In doing so, he discovered one so bizarre, he immediately turned it over to DOI. It detailed the water police investigation of a peaceful Muslim community consisting of a few hundred men, women, and children who had sought solitude in the northern woods.

The new chief of the water cops asked himself what connection these Muslims might have with potential pollution of the water supply, which, officially at least, was the sole reason for the existence of the water police. Bob Frank, DOI's deputy inspector general for the Environmental Protection Department, asked himself exactly that.

He took out a map and studied the location of the Muslim community. It was two miles from the nearest reservoir, on land that sloped away from the reservoir site. So involuntary pollution of the water supply was not an issue.

That left Frank with the question of whether Sgt. James Van Tyle, the water police officer who, it turned out, had begun the investigation of the Muslims, thought the Muslims might be attempting to pollute the city water supply on purpose. If that were their aim, their method of doing so would certainly have stood out in the history of crime. Most criminals attempt to flee the scene of the crime, not settle their spouses and children in a fifty-five-acre compound near the crime scene.

But even this speculative counterargument goes way beyond the facts because not a single person in the area had alleged that the Muslims were attempting to pollute the water supply.

What Van Tyle did allege, when Frank interrogated him, was this: someone who lived near the Muslim compound had told Van Tyle that an employee of a federal law-enforcement agency had left his card with him and requested that he forward to him the license plate numbers of vehicles driving in and out of the Muslim compound. Van Tyle called this federal law enforcement officer several times, he told Frank, but that officer never returned his calls.

That was enough for Van Tyle. As he very accurately told Frank, since the water police didn't actually perform the job assigned to them, "we just wait to be dispatched" by local police agencies. As a result, "we get bored just driving around."

So Van Tyle ordered a full-scale investigation of the Muslim compound. His first step was to check the local newspaper for anything it had published about the Muslims. And there it was, in a February 1988 issue: "Sunni Muslims Found Peaceloving Community."

Van Tyle's next step, interview the superintendent of the local school district. If the superintendent had told Van Tyle the Muslims didn't send their kids to school, the sergeant would have had an actual allegation of illegal activity to work with, or, possibly, an excuse to stage a raid on the compound.

However, the superintendent told Van Tyle that the Muslims sent the boys to school and the boys were exemplary students. He noted that the Muslims insisted on educating the girls themselves at the compound, but said that several inspections by school personnel had indicated that the education of the girls was being properly conducted, as required by state law.

Van Tyle checked with the town clerk and discovered that the Muslims were paying their taxes. He checked with the local building department, which told him that the structures at the compound had passed all required inspections.

Then came the sort of break in the case investigators dream of. The Fire Department reported that a blaze had occurred a few months before in a trailer in the compound. When a neighbor called the Fire Department to report it—the Muslims hadn't bothered to call the department, because they were fighting it successfully themselves—the neighbor had heard what he thought was live ammunition going off. Moreover, the Muslims had refused to allow the Fire Department into the compound, since they had put the fire out themselves.

While the Muslims were bringing the fire under control, however, the fire chief made an important observation. He saw "approximately 150 to 200 black men and women running around the area." The Muslims were black. The new water police administrator volunteered to DOI that this was probably why the water cops under his predecessor had begun the investigation in the first place.

Van Tyle had heard what he needed. The water police had to get into that compound. Using the excuse that a neighbor had complained about dogs running loose in the area, Van Tyle and his men entered the compound to pick up what information they could.

Once inside, the sergeant and his men recorded all the license plate numbers they saw and later checked the numbers with the Department of Motor Vehicles and the sheriff's office. They then checked the names of the vehicle owners with the State Police Information Network. The water cops ignored the network requirement that an official criminal investigation case number be used when making such a check. The water cops didn't have a case number because they'd had no acceptable reason for opening the investigation in the first place.

The network told the water cops that none of the cars checked were stolen and none of the drivers had criminal records or were wanted on any charges. Van Tyle decided on a flyover. He circumvented the water police lack of an air auxiliary unit by persuading an employee of the Environmental Protection Department to fly him over the compound in the employee's private aircraft so Van Tyle could photograph the compound from the air. He saw nothing suspicious.

The next step was to enlist a member of one of the local police forces—a man who wanted to join the water police—to enter the compound, posing as a helper on a garbage truck. While inside, this officer searched the remains of the trailer that had been involved in the fire and discovered a notebook in the ruins, which he placed under his jacket and removed from the property. He also spoke into a tape recorder that he hid in one of his pockets as he moved about the Muslim compound. He later gave the notebook to Van Tyle, who kept it in an unlocked storage locker at water police headquarters until it was eventually lost. As a result of his participation in the investigation, this officer was, soon thereafter, allowed to join the water force.

A couple of weeks later, the real garbageman, in the process of hauling off the innards of a discarded dishwasher he'd been hired to remove from the compound, recovered a box of spent shell casings from the dishwasher's innards. He gave the shell casings to the water cops, who put them in the same locker in which they had stored the notebook.

Van Tyle called the cartridges a significant find. When Frank asked him what connection existed between investigating the Muslims and protecting the reservoirs from pollution, Van Tyle put his hand on the recovered casings and declared, "In order to contaminate the reservoirs, you must have the will to do so. This stuff tells me they had the will."

Encouraged by the appearance of this evidence, Van Tyle arranged for a second flyover. This time, since the case had expanded, Van Tyle arranged with a local Air National Guard unit for a helicopter flight over the compound. The sergeant told DOI the purpose of taking this second set of aerial photos was "to learn the lay of the land in case we had to go in." Van Tyle didn't indicate why he'd want to go in. But as an apparent cover for his mission, the sergeant combined the second overfly with a search for marijuana on a nearby strip of city-owned land. None was found.

It was at this point that DOI intervened. The investigation of the Muslims, DOI concluded in its report, "was the product of irrational fears acted upon by a police unit suffering from inadequate training, ignorance of the law, poor management, supervisory paralysis, and boredom" and "demonstrated a breakdown of acceptable law enforcement practices and a disregard for constitutional safeguards."

Once again, Commissioner Shepard, at Frank's urging, recommended that the water police be combined with the watershed inspectors, who actually worked to protect the city's water supply from polluters. Her recommendation was ignored.

DEATH ON THE INSTALLMENT PLAN

Let us cross the river and rest under the trees.
—Last words, Stonewall Jackson, 1863

DOI dealt with relatively high-level crooks: working people as opposed to dope dealers, and white-collar workers rather than laborers. One of our more intriguing cases, however, dealt with a white-collar city employee who was intimately connected with a syringe-shooting, track-making, head-nodding, vacant-eyed, permanently constipated addict. However, this odd couple, bizarre as they were, weren't the criminals in the case. The city employees who preyed on the fruit of their affair—they were the bad guys.

Don Milstein, the white-collar employee involved, took a clerk-ing job with the city Finance Department in 1979. The pay was-n't all that good, but the benefits were excellent.

After settling in at his new job, Don looked closely at the rest of his life. He lived in the Bronx with his family. But his family was eating at him. Taking that long subway ride from official Man-hattan to that middle-class enclave in the Bronx every day to sleep and eat with people he didn't love didn't appeal to him anymore. But since he didn't like living alone, he stayed put.

Then he met Gloria. Gloria Rivera. In Don's eyes, she was everything a woman should be: willing, beautiful, undemand-ing. She was also fond of recreational drugs. He couldn't resist. After a few unbelievably passionate encounters, he decided to make a change. He moved out on his family in the Bronx and moved in with Gloria in an apartment on Avenue D in Man-hattan.

This neighborhood is occasionally referred to as "Alphabet City" because the avenues are lettered rather than numbered. It's also referred to as "The End of the World," because a large num-ber of people have the feeling they're stepping off the edge of the earth once they cross First Avenue, heading east. While there are many responsible and civic-minded people who live in Alphabet City, Gloria's incredibly long arrest record indicated she wasn't one of them. But God, did she and Don hit if off. For seven years, with the money Don made and Gloria's beauty, they lived the life. They lived the life.

For all his wild living, Don retained his middle-class ways. He reported faithfully to his job at the Finance Department every morning and came home to Gloria and her needle collection every evening. Gloria made him happy. And Don was a grateful man who paid his debts. He tried as best he could to make Gloria happy in this life, but he knew that her arrest record and her habit of nodding off before she removed the syringe from her arm wouldn't help her much in the job market if he was gone. So he took steps to provide for her after his death. When benefit forms were passed out at work, he requested that his pension contributions be transferred to his death-benefit account. On that part of the form where he was asked to name and identify the recipient of the benefit in the event of his death, he filled in "Gloria Rivera, common-law wife."

He kept working. He and Gloria kept partying. The pension money kept piling up. The present was ecstatically happy, the future warm and secure. Then, one cold day in December 1986, Don died. It was over.

Don had told Gloria about the death benefit, of course, but Gloria was more of a sensualist than an intellectual, so she forgot all about it.

Although Gloria wasn't looking for Don's death benefit, the benefit was looking for her. The retirement system's death division sent Gloria one registered letter after another, informing her that Don's death benefit, swollen to $76,779.15 as a result of his pension contributions being added during his years of city employment, was available to her. All she had to do was claim it. The letters were all returned "Addressee Unknown." A lot of people in Alphabet City want to be unknown. A lot of them succeed.

The death division staffers even went to the trouble of sending registered letters to Don's family in the Bronx, requesting information about Gloria's whereabouts. These letters were delivered, but never answered. Don's family wasn't too interested in providing the city with information about Ms. Rivera. Don's money stayed in the vaults of the retirement system.

Meanwhile, Gloria stayed on drugs. She had loved Don and missed him, so she increased her daily dosage in an effort to forget him. She almost succeeded, staying doped up for another few years until a death certificate was issued in her name in February 1989.

Then, in October, eight months after her death certificate was issued, Gloria wrote the retirement system asking politely whether there might be any benefits due her because of poor Don's demise. When the death division joyfully wrote back, informing her of the money available to her and sending her a request-for-benefit form, she returned it, signed and notarized. No one noticed that the social security number written on it was wrong. The death division immediately sent her the money.

All was quiet until 1991, when a security officer at the American Savings Bank called DOI. His call was routed to Inspector General Brian Foley, whose office was responsible for the retirement system. Foley, tall, pale, thin, and phlegmatic, listened with growing interest as the security officer told him that the bank had evidence that one of its tellers, Wendy Clarke, and one of its depositors, Gloria Rivera, might have conspired to defraud the city retirement system. The matter had come to the security officer's attention when a routine bank audit had turned up the information that Clarke, the teller, had transferred interest payments that had been automatically deposited into Rivera's account into Clarke's personal account. This act violated bank regulations, and, in fact, was thievery. The bank had fired Clarke.

As was standard in such cases, bank auditors then reviewed the records of the Rivera account. They discovered that although the account had been opened in November 1989 with a $100 deposit, the bulk of the money deposited in the account, $76,779.15, had arrived in the form of a death division check made out to Gloria Rivera. But surprisingly, although the money had all been withdrawn from the account, none of it had been withdrawn by Gloria. Cashier's checks had been made out to Roxanne Scott, Joyce Clark, Yvette Wills-Brown, and Victoria Gordon. A large portion of the money had been transferred directly from the Rivera account into Teller Clarke's account.

Inspector General Foley and DOI Investigator Marci Serber immediately subpoenaed the bank records belonging to Scott, Clark, Wills-Brown, and Gordon and researched their identities. They soon made several interesting discoveries. One was that Gloria Rivera was really dead. The second was that Wills-Brown was a retirement system accountant and Gordon a retirement-system benefit examiner, who, in order to better herself, was studying law at night. And both Wills-Brown and Gordon had once worked together at the retirement system. In the death division.

While neither Don nor Gloria had involved their families in the accumulation of the death benefit, Accountant Wills-Brown had moved dramatically in the opposite direction. She had involved three generations of hers in the dispersal of that benefit. Teller Clarke was her niece. Roxanne Scott was her sister. And at least one senior citizen got into the act: Joyce Clark, her mother.

Some DOI investigators thought it was nice of Wills-Brown to share the money with her family the way she did. Others, somewhat more cynical, saw her apparent generosity as a way to ensure that each recipient, if caught, would receive only a minimum penalty because of the relatively small amount of money involved. However, the stolen money wasn't kept completely in the family. Gordon, not related to anybody else, got her cut, and I find it hard to believe the notary who validated the deceased Gloria Rivera's signature on the request-for-benefit form didn't get something in return.

Since Gordon, Scott, Clark, Clarke, and Wills-Brown all had endorsed their checks before they cashed them, as required, and the bank had evidence of Teller Clarke's transfers, the case against them wasn't that difficult to make. Aside from the trail of cashier's checks, the handwriting on the benefit request form, which purported to be Gloria's, was actually Rosanne Scott's.

All those involved were arrested and convicted. Yvette Wills-Brown and Victoria Gordon were sentenced to one to three years in prison each and Roxanne Scott to one year. Wendy Clarke, the bank teller, was wrist-slapped with five years probation. The City Law Department, as is standard in such cases, sued for the return of all moneys stolen. The retirement system promised to reform its procedures so that nothing like this would ever happen again.

As for Don and Gloria, they were probably laughing together, somewhere.

CHAPTER 14

"DO YOU WANT TO FUCK THE MAYOR?"

"But darling," Daisy interrupted. "Tangier's a one-horse town that happens to have its own government. And you know damned well that all government lives on corruption. I don't care what sort—socialist, totalitarian, democratic—it's all the same. Naturally in a little place like this you come in contact with the government constantly. God knows, it's inevitable. And so you're always conscious of the corruption.—From Let It Come Down, *by Paul Bowles (Santa Rosa: Black Sparrow Press, 1990)*

Working as a flack for a city agency that investigated other city agencies, including city hall itself, can only be described as a schizophrenic experience. Every single one of my colleagues, the spokespeople for other city agencies, did their very best to make their bosses and their departments look good. They tried to persuade reporters to write or broadcast positive stories about the agency they worked for or the personnel in it and tried to kill or tone down any bad stories.

I certainly did the best I could to kill or tone down bad stories that might be written about DOI. I didn't feel uneasy about doing this, since there is no truth. All truths are merely different versions of an event. Therefore, I attempted to provide DOI's view of events to every single reporter who wanted to know it or whom I thought should know it.

It was when I was trying to bring DOI's achievements to public attention that things got a bit complicated. In most cases, whenever DOI did well—by arresting forty-eight corrupt city officials, for instance—those city officials did badly, by being arrested and listening as the news was broadcast to the world.

So, while my fellow flacks were as one with the general purpose of city flackery—to make the city look good—I was out on my own, trying to make DOI look good, often, unavoidably, at some other department's or flack's expense.

For other flacks, getting a call from me just after an arrest was not a pleasant experience. At Shepard's instructions and under her supervision, I would tell my fellow flack about the arrests, inform him or her that we were going to issue a press release about the arrests—calling them to the attention of the public—and wait for the groaning to cease. Then I would ask the flack to obtain a statement from the head of the department whose officials or employees we had just arrested. I would include the statement in DOI's press release as the victimized department's defense, but there was no way these defenses could sound anything but lame. Whatever they actually said, they always sounded like variations on "I'm shocked! Shocked! To learn that illegal gambling is going on here!"

Realizing this, flacks from gored departments often pressed me to issue a joint release to give the impression that both departments had investigated the case. When the department had indeed helped in the investigation, we acceded to this request. Otherwise, we did not. Sometimes the departments would put out their own press releases justifying themselves and issue them to the same reporters who had received the DOI release. None of this did much good in terms of first-day coverage, although it did make the heads of the gored departments feel better. Reporters like scandal, and DOI provided it. The pathetic defenses thrown up by the arrestees or those who hired or supervised them were buried at the bottom of the news stories.

On a few occasions, flacks at victimized departments tried to sell second-day stories to the newspapers about alleged flaws in DOI's investigation. Shepard and I fought back against these stories, which were the bane of our existence, with every weapon we could muster. When they appeared, they sent Shepard through the roof. I comforted myself with the belief, however, that the scandal, not some minor screwup in the investigation, mattered most to the general public. But, as someone once said, no one lives in a big city, they live in a neighborhood. And the neighborhood Shepard lived in was the city hall neighborhood, where alleged DOI screwups were the stuff of gleeful, whispered hallway conversations.

But city hall screwups—and criminal activities—were the stuff of gleeful, whispered hallway conversations at DOI, as were occasional city hall efforts to stop me from publicizing the hall's misdeeds or to punish me after I did so. Frank Ling was the subject of such efforts at punishment.

As far as DOI investigators could determine, Frank Ling, a Hong Kong resident, was admitted to the U.S. in 1976, attended a small college, and then studied at a big city university until 1981. Subsequently, he worked with and for Chinese-American community groups in the city, then hooked up with the city government as a community relations worker for the Sanitation

Department. Talented and diligent, he was by 1990 a major player in the Dinkins administration. As assistant director of the Mayor's Community Action Unit, Ling organized Dinkins's successful series of town meetings that boded so well for the administration in its early days.

His salary at Sanitation had been relatively modest, which gave him a tremendous advantage—it wasn't large enough to trigger a DOI check of his past. But when Ling rose to his relatively high city post, he became prominent enough to be the subject of such an investigation, known as a background check.

These exhaustive checks, performed on the pasts of all high-level city officials—and many not-so-high officials in certain categories, including all of DOI's own employees—were a major DOI headache and function. Their function, of course, was to prevent the city from hiring people who weren't what they claimed to be. They were a headache because they were so thorough and required so many checks with so many other agencies that when a background check uncovered a fraud, the cry usually was not "Good work!" but "What the fuck took you so long?"

What made it look worse was that those being checked were allowed by city policy to take and hold office while the background check was being done. If this hadn't been allowed, DOI would have been forced to expand its small background unit to gargantuan size or many officials of any new administration would not have been allowed to take office until their mayor's reelection campaign began.

Ling's background check was initiated, therefore, after he took office. It began routinely, with a check of his educational claims. DOI's background checkers, following standard procedure, asked the university to confirm in writing that it had awarded Ling the degree he claimed. The university wrote that it had no information on Ling. But record mix-ups were common, so Frank O'Regan, a special investigator, asked Ling to bring in the degree itself.

What Ling brought in was a photocopy of his alleged degree. The investigator, usually a friendly fellow, refused to accept it. He demanded the "degree, the degree, the degree."

Ling stalled for weeks. He claimed the degree was in a safety-deposit box in a bank in an outlying suburb and that he just didn't have time to drive out and get it. When O'Regan kept demanding to see it, Ling presented a letter from the university registrar, on university stationery, signed by the registrar herself, explaining "To Whom It May Concern" that Ling had, indeed, earned his degree and that the university was in the process of sending him a new certificate to replace the one he'd lost.

O'Regan visited the registrar to double-check the letter. The university registrar was shocked to see the letter the investigator slammed down on her desk, since, although it had her name at the bottom and was on her stationery, she hadn't written it.

When O'Regan came back with his report that indicated a top city official had not only lied but had forged a document to support his lie, his superiors decided to look more closely at the rest of Ling's record.

Ling had submitted to DOI a photocopy of a perfectly acceptable-looking driver's license. However, when DOI officials checked with the appropriate officials elsewhere, they discovered that the license had been issued by LCS (Ling's Computer System) rather than the DMV (Department of Motor Vehicles).

On checking with the federal Immigration and Naturalization Service, they discovered that Ling's extremely official looking Certificate of Naturalization was also, in fact, of LCS issue.

His voter registration card came from the same source.

The deeper DOI looked into Ling's file, the more it began to resemble a photocopied onion as one fake layer of skin after another peeled away and disintegrated. Had Ling ever lived in Hong Kong, which he claimed as his pre-U.S. residence? Was his name really Frank Ling? Who was "Frank Ling"? O'Regan's superiors were tempted to send him to Asia to find out.

DOI's limited budget prevented them from doing that, but they could do something else. In conjunction with the Immigration and Naturalization Service and the U.S. Attorney's office, they recommended that DOI arrest Ling on federal felony charges for forging his naturalization papers.

Commissioner approval was required before any arrest could be made. Signed arrest authorization forms were, in fact, prestigious documents, not only for legal purposes, but because they indicated the commissioner had approved of the work of the investigator who presented her with the form. A signed form indicated the extent to which Shepard was willing to authorize a rather disruptive interruption of an individual's life and a potentially large risk to the department's reputation if the arrest was a bum one, on the basis of that subordinate's work.

Shepard approved the arrest, but told the investigators and me not to release any word of it until Ling had been asked to cooperate with us in investigating any corruption higher up in city hall. In keeping with this plan, DOI detectives arrested Ling unobtrusively one fine morning as he left home for work. They took him to a federal courthouse for booking. Unfortunately, reporter M. P. McQueen of *New York Newsday* spotted Ling in the courthouse lobby with the detectives. She asked what was going on, since the situation smacked of an arrest and the arrest of a city hall totem would be a big story.

The detectives, fast thinkers both of them, came up on the spot with the outlandish cover story that, no, Ling wasn't under arrest, he was merely being escorted to the courthouse to help translate the testimony of a Chinese-speaking witness in an important federal trial. As an on-the-run cover story, this rated an "A" in anyone's grade book, but McQueen knew there were plenty of

Chinese translators available and the probability that a city official would be required to translate at a federal trial was very low. She bought the cover story for as long as it took her to get back to her computer screen and write a news story saying DOI was investigating Ling.

McQueen was responsible enough to call and ask me, among other questions, if we wanted Ling's arrest kept quiet for some reason. I promised to call her back, then suggested to Shepard, as I had suggested on several occasions involving other reporters and other cases, that we ask McQueen if she could please hold her story until we had used Ling as an agent for awhile.

Shepard refused, as she did every time I suggested this course of action to her. This was partly because Shepard was the straightest woman I've ever known. She loved following the rules, and the rules were that we didn't talk about arrests either off or on the record until we were ready to do so. She also didn't want to be in the position of owing McQueen a favor. And, finally, and mistakenly, she believed McQueen wouldn't be able to write her story about Ling's arrest unless we confirmed it, a mistake she and numerous other public officials often made and continue to make. A few newspapers—the *New York Times* being one—almost always wait for what one reporter called "the sacrament of confirmation," but many others, including McQueen's paper in this case, did not.

If Ling had had a chance to cooperate with us, maybe even wear a wire, he would have been a great undercover agent. He was certainly a great liar. Having been arrested, and then released on his own recognizance, he was back at his City Hall desk that afternoon, in plenty of time to deny to McQueen, with some heat when she came around to his office to check on him, that he had ever been arrested, either that morning or ever in his life. He even went so far as to ask her indignantly what he would be doing back at his office if he had been taken into custody.

But it was too late for such bravado. McQueen wrote her story, her newspaper printed it—ending Ling's usefulness as a potential amateur investigator—and embarrassing city hall to the extent that Ling was shortly relieved of his duties.

We had been hoping to keep Ling's arrest a state secret while he worked undercover for us. But once McQueen's story appeared, we decided we might as well issue a press release about the entire affair. Somewhat naively, we titled the press release "DOI Arrests High City Official for Submitting Fraudulent Documents." We also mentioned, in the first paragraph of the release, that Ling had submitted a bogus certificate of naturalization to city officials in order to obtain his city job.

The first reaction to the release came from Leland Jones, Mayor Dinkins's press secretary. I was sitting calmly in my chair. The sun was slanting through my narrow eighteenth-floor window, my computer was humming, and a steaming cup of coffee was sitting on the desk in front of me. All was well in my little world.

Then, the phone rang.

Since my secretary was down the hall, I picked it up myself. "Benjaminson," I said. "DO YOU WANT TO FUCK THE MAYOR?" a voice on the other end asked. "DO YOU WANT TO FUCK THE MAYOR? DO YOU WANT TO FUCK THE MAYOR? DO YOU WANT TO FUCK THE MAYOR? " I recognized Lee Jones's hysterical tones. Weeks later it occurred to me that the appropriate response would have been "No, Lee, I'm straight. I don't want to fuck the mayor," but all I did, I'm sure, was burble.

Jones spent the next fifteen minutes informing me that much of the mayor's political support came from immigrant groups, and the very thought that DOI was going after illegal immigrants would undercut that support, destroy the mayor, and ruin the entire city and everyone in it. He assured me that very soon I'd be spending my days doing nothing but answering outraged phone calls from immigrants and immigrant-group representatives. Then he slammed the phone down.

I was a bit shaken, although I didn't work for Jones and therefore couldn't be disciplined by him. I was certain Shepard would stand up for me. (She did.) And, I thought, why should DOI care about the mayor and the political support he may or may not get in the next election? We were an independent investigative agency, not part of his campaign apparatus. The fact that I could have thought this at all and not burst into nonstop giggling showed the profound effect that Shepard had had on DOI.

Jones's estimate of the reaction the release would elicit was a bit off the mark. I spent weeks tabulating the number of angry phone calls I received from immigrants and immigrant groups protesting DOI's actions in the Ling case. Here, for students of politics, immigration policy, and interaction among high-level city agencies, is the carefully totaled number of such calls my staff and I tabulated: 0.

Later on in the administration, when we arrested a prominent Korean immigrant in another case, we got one call—from a Korean-language newspaper that wanted a picture of the official so they could display the story on her arrest more prominently. Perhaps Jones's judgment was a bit lacking.

Ling could have been sentenced to thirteen years in jail and a $750,000 fine but was eventually sentenced to a $2,000 fine, two years probation, a $25 special assessment, 300 hours of community service, and the strong possibility of deportation. But to where?

THE CASE OF THE BANKRUPT BUSINESS COMMISSIONER

Sunshine is the best disinfectant.
—Anonymous

I struggled so hard to get stories in the papers about DOI's tri-
umphs—and failed so often, partly due to my own inadequacies
and partly due to the abilities of my competitors—that I felt a
tremendous kinship with DOI investigations that came asunder.

However, even when you win in the short run, you may lose
in the long run. And it's generally difficult to have a permanent
effect on things. Steve Pasichow, one of whose duties was inves-

tigating corrupt privately operated social-service agencies for DOI, once complained to me that even if he succeeded in jailing the head of one of these agencies, the perp would leave the running of it in the hands of a brother-in-law while he did his time, then take it over again when his term was up. Occasionally, DOI and other law enforcement agencies would react to such a setback by moving to have the private agency or crook banned from bidding on future city business. But then the crook would reorganize the same company under another name with a different executive's name on the stationery and try for the golden apple once again.

While Wallace Ford, Mayor Dinkins's commissioner of the newly formed Department of Business Services, wasn't one of those people, he was a closely related type—someone who leapt happily from one disaster to another, each disaster a bigger fiasco than the former, with reputation and income not only intact, but enhanced.

As head of the State Mortgage Agency in the early 1960s, before he became involved with city government, Ford had appointed a convicted bank robber as his assistant. State officials later discovered "irregularities" that cost the agency $100,000. Ford was asked to leave.

But he emerged in 1985 into a hospitable environment. Many entrepreneurs were trying to get rich during the eighties. What distinguished the eighties from other periods in American history, however, was that many of them were succeeding. So Ford figured he'd give it a try. He and a fellow Harvard Law School alum attempted to buy three California banks and savings-and-loan operations. But they could never quite come up with the money. (Ford's fellow alumnus, Ernest Lee Brazil, later pleaded guilty to grand larceny in California for taking more than $1 million from an investor under false pretenses.)

During the maneuvering involved, the Federal Home Loan Bank Board criticized Ford for lacking "prudent business judg-

ment." California state bank regulators questioned the "compe-
tence, experience, integrity, and resources" of the shell company,
Eagle Ventures, which Ford was using as a vehicle to attempt the
savings-and-loan purchases.

Soon afterward, Ford was appointed head of the city's Department of Business Services.

DOI's attention was first drawn to him when one of Ford's
former employees sent us a complaint a few months after she had
heard that Ford had been appointed commissioner of Business
Services. The employee, a savings-and-loan acquisitions expert,
said in a notarized affidavit that she had been employed by Eagle
for six months to help Ford acquire one of the institutions he had
his eye on. Ford had promised her, verbally, a salary of $90,000
per year, she said.

She was a little uneasy about accepting such a promise without documentation and spent her spare time over the next several months, while working full time for Ford, trying to wring a
written salary agreement out of him. Pleading an extremely busy
schedule, Ford finally agreed "to provide a written commitment
which he suggested he would write during a flight from California" to the East Coast, according to her affidavit.

He did so and gave her the document, but even in the document, her compensation remained "deferred." Ford then
promised her "equity participation" in the still-to-be acquired
thrift as well as in Eagle, "expressing his appreciation of my understanding of Eagle Ventures's 'cash flow problems,'" she wrote.

She continued to work, on faith. I suppose you could fault
her for this, but Ford was impressive, and overwhelmingly sin-
cere, in person. That's probably how he had impressed Dinkins,
who, rather courtly himself, was inclined to see the best in people whatever the evidence against them.

Ford told the woman that he and the controlling shareholder
in Eagle "both agreed that the monies owed me at that point were

a personal commitment that stood apart from any other Eagle corporate debt and that they ensured its payment in full notwithstanding the lack of financing for 'other EVI debt.' When I was not satisfied with that verbal commitment," she continued in her affidavit, "and expressed further concern over my personal financial situation that developed as a result of my involvement with Eagle Ventures, Mr. Ford assured me that he would personally pay me."

When she expressed doubt, "Mr. Ford again assured me that I would be paid, requesting that I stick it out with Eagle Ventures, reminding me that they were also involved in alternative acquisition efforts which would become a source of cash flow to pay me. When I questioned him yet further he informed me that he had listed for sale his personal residence for the purpose of satisfying his personal debt . . . "

On June 1, 1989, still unpaid, she resigned from Eagle. Her resignation included a summary of the money owed her, more than $50,000. During the last week of June, Ford told her he would make full restitution that same week. Nothing happened.

On July 12, Ford called her and suggested lunch. On July 19, they met. At the lunch, she said, "Mr. Ford proceeded to offer an alternative to waiting for the proceeds from the sale of his residence and suggested that he was expecting a positive outcome from litigation between Eagle Ventures and Peninsula Savings and that could be the source of the payment . . . He promised to call me the following Friday with a progress report and 'to keep in much closer contact.'" He then reminded her that "It's not IF but WHEN I can pay you."

The WHEN wasn't July 26, July 31, or August 3, when she tried to reach him by phone. When she finally did reach him on August 4, he said he'd check with his attorney and call her back later in the day. He did not. When she reached him again on August 7 and protested, he called her the following day and left a message indicating he had nothing to report but would call again the following day. He didn't. He called her again on August 23 indicating that he would have more information for her in two weeks, according to her affidavit.

That was the last she heard from him for eight months. On May 7, 1991, he assured her over the phone that he still intended to pay her. When she pointed out that he was by then receiving a large salary as a commissioner, "he responded by offering to call me weekly to report as to his personal financial situation as it related to the timing for the payment of the money he owed to me. I told him that I was not interested in receiving weekly telephone calls from him, but that I expected him to send me written correspondence confirming our telephone conversation. He became quite indignant." That was the last she ever heard from him, she wrote.

On January 26, 1990, the labor commissioner of the state of California entered a judgment in her favor for the $50,068 Eagle Ventures owed her. In April 1990, a New York State Supreme Court judge awarded another claimant, an investor in Ford's projects, a $489,000 judgment against Eagle. It was just when Ford had reached this low point in his fortunes that Mayor Dinkins appointed him to high city office.

After reading these documents, I figured we had a case for sure, and a nice juicy one at that, considering Ford's high rank. After all, here was a major city official who apparently had admitted a legal and legitimate financial obligation that he refused to pay and which had been endorsed as a legitimate debt by a governmental authority. Brian Foley, the DOI inspector general who was assigned to investigate the complaint, felt the same way. But after sending one of his investigators to interview the employee, and determining that the unpaid judgment was her only complaint against Ford, a tiny but decisive technicality emerged. The judgment was against Eagle Ventures, not against Ford. "It's a corporate debt," Foley told me, shrugging. "That's why people incorporate, to protect themselves from these things." The company itself? It was out of business and thus couldn't pay. In fact, Foley said, it wasn't even worth interviewing Ford. Foley closed the case.

Last I heard, Ford's secretary wouldn't lend him lunch money, which he requested from her frequently, because he never paid it back.

THERE WAS A YOUNG LADY NAMED CHOI . . .

There was a young lady named Choi
Who gave DOE little joy;
She cooked all the books,
Neglected her looks
And almost pulled off a trompe l'oeil.
—DOI doggerel

I was just about up to here with crooked civil servants when Steve Pasichow came up behind me at a Monday morning meeting, which was held, as usual, in the glass-walled conference room near the top of the DOI tower. "I've got something to tell you," he said. The something turned out to be Christina Choi.

Choi would have been an heroic figure under the Giuliani administration. She was, after all, the leader of a privately owned organization that performed services the government wanted performed, and she didn't employ public servants to do so.

Her private, nonprofit organization, Korean Manpower Development, had provided vocational, literacy, employment, and after-school programs to the city's Korean community for only a few hundred thousand dollars a year in city, state, and federal funds. In many people's eyes, Choi's way was the way of the future: privately owned organizations, staffed with vigorous, hard-working employees, providing, at relatively little cost, services formerly provided by highly paid, lethargic civil servants.

She recently had been appointed second-in-command of the city's Department of Employment. But Pasichow had heard something about her conduct as head of the private agency she had run before being appointed that didn't sound good. He also had found out that she was dying of cancer, which meant we had to move quickly if we were going to nab her before the Big Guy did.

All Pasichow needed to know was that Choi's actual income was vastly higher than the not-so-impressive salary she was being paid by Korean Manpower Development. He and his investigators immediately began a thorough check of her bank, tax, real estate, income, and charge-card records. He found that she, indeed, had had her private-sector hand very deep in the public-sector till. After a few months of going over bank and agency records, he discovered where her extra money had been coming from.

Choi had started out by paying herself her own salary twice, under two different names. Then, not satisfied with doubling her own salary, she began paying her sister for work the sister didn't perform. Her sister, who was supposedly providing computer training to KMD enrollees, was actually waitressing in a Manhattan restaurant. When her sister asked Choi why KMD kept sending her large checks in the mail when she didn't do anything for the agency, Choi told her that it would be good for KMD if she just kept receiving and endorsing the checks and sending them back to Choi, who would, Choi said, redeposit them in the agency's account. Instead of doing so, however, Choi and a coconspirator, her roommate, opened twenty different bank accounts at ten different banks and deposited Choi's sister's check, along with many other purloined ducats, in them.

Pretty soon, though, Choi realized she wasn't going to get rich as quick as she wanted to this way. Land and buildings, that's where the real money is, she thought. So she and her roommate bought a building and leased it to KMD at more than twice the going rate. To make the lease presentable—after all, she was renting the building from herself—she used her Korean name as the renter and her Anglicized name as the rentee.

Within a short while, the checks from Choi's various illicit KMD sources had fattened her bank accounts by approximately $400,000. It might be worthwhile to stop at this point and ask how just one modestly sized service-providing private-sector agency working under contract to one of twenty or so city government agencies could accumulate that much money. The answer is simple. The city government spends $3 billion a year. I believe it should spend even more. Look around you, and you can see what there is to be done. But spending any large sum leads to a lot of stray crumbs.

It might also be worthwhile to ask what Choi needed the money for. Or, for that matter, what many crooks at her level needed the money for. The answer is she didn't need it. She was addicted to money and had to have more and more of it to keep her thrill level high. If she hadn't been caught, she wouldn't have retired or built a dream house or bought an island or anything extravagant. She just would have kept on stealing larger and larger amounts.

Choi was so successful at stealing in the private sector that after a few years of looting KMD, she was ready to move on to the big time. She wangled herself the appointment as assistant commissioner of the Employment Department, the source of some of KMD's funding. She was only in office a short while before DOI arrested her, so all she was able to do in her new job was continue to loot KMD. But who knows what schemes heated up in her brain as she sat at her desk at the Department of Employment, partly responsible for an annual budget that dwarfed her former agency's?

Pasichow, once he had uncovered the details of Choi's scheme, also saw that a portion of the money she had stolen was federal. Knowing the federal penalties would be more severe for the crimes Choi had committed, he called in the FBI and had that agency arrest her.

Of course, at that point the real war began—who would get the credit for the arrest? Now that Choi was in the bag, every-one wanted in. Out of nowhere, the U.S. attorney's office, the peo-ple who would prosecute Choi in court, told me they planned to issue a release about the arrest, ignoring the historic interde-partmental agreement that when a perp is arrested on a criminal complaint, as Choi was, the arresting organization gets to put out the release. When the perp is arrested on an indictment, the pros-ecuting agency puts out the release.

It wasn't long before my equivalent at the FBI heard about the U.S. attorney's plan and contacted me. We agreed that I would put out a joint FBI-DOI release as quickly as possible on the day of the arrest and arrange for the name of the head of the FBI bureau in New York to be the first one mentioned.

Whose name would go first in a press release was a matter of tremendous importance to many law enforcement officials. The top dog gets the credit, they thought. Which was true as far as it went.

But, at the risk of sounding demented, please allow me to bring up an opposing theory much discussed in "public infor-mation" circles. The stationery on which a release is issued is more important than whose name is first. And most important of all is who the reporter hears it from first, especially if he hears it early. Then he'll feel he owes his early informer one for doing him a favor and will try to help that person out by naming his agency in the story. I often told reporters which perps had been arrested and why hours before the actual release went out with its much debated first sentence bearing the names and titles of the heads of the agencies involved exactly in the agreed-on order. By the time these intricate productions were released, however, the reporters didn't care. Their stories were already written.

In any case, that strategy worked this time. Later on, the U.S. attorney issued his own release, but by then it was too late. DOI got the credit in the *Times* and the *Post*. The FBI got some credit in one of the city's Korean-language papers. And the U.S. attorney got no credit anywhere.

Then came the final bout. How would we convict Choi before the iceman cometh? In a way, she made it easy for us. Before the FBI and DOI interrogated her sister, she called her sister and told her to lie when asked what she did for the agency. The sister complied, but then, after the agents left, had second thoughts and asked them to return, at which point she told them the true story.

This left an opening for DOI to ask that Choi be charged with tampering with a witness and making a false statement on her income tax return, both somewhat peripheral in terms of the reason we'd arrested Choi in the first place but, significantly, both charges to which Choi agreed to plead guilty. Apparently she considered admitting to these charges less shameful than to admit to the other crimes she had been accused of. Her guilty plea on these charges allowed us to recapture the $400,000 she had stolen and return it to the city treasury. Because of Choi's illness, the judge departed from federal guidelines and sentenced the dying woman to five years on probation, allowing her to live out her last days in relative peace and relative poverty.

Choi's death was, of course, unrelated to DOI's investigation of her, but that wasn't the case with some other DOI targets, including Alfredo Mathew, Jr., as well as a city plumbing inspector who shall go unnamed.

The body of Mathew, the superintendent of a South Bronx community school district, was found in 1993 in an Albany motel room with two plastic bags taped around his head.

DOI was on the trail of Mathew and three of his former coworkers because we strongly suspected him of masterminding a conspiracy that stole $185,000 from two antipoverty agencies with which he was associated before he became superintendent. Mathew and his coconspirators, we believed, laundered the money in a dummy company set up for that purpose and funneled about $10,000 of it, illegally, to politicians. Some of the money the three men and one woman stole was spent on restaurant meals, airline flights, home furnishings, flowers, toys, clothing, and tickets to sports events. Mathew and his cohorts were supposed to be using the money to help poverty-stricken elderly people who were unable to care for themselves, children who needed day care, and homeless AIDS patients.

Although Mathew's apparent suicide occurred soon after he had spilled his guts to DOI investigators, no one felt particularly bad about his death. The investigators were just doing their jobs, and Mathew's cooperation could easily be seen as an attempt to unburden himself of guilt.

Feelings at the agency were somewhat more mixed when a victim of Parkinson's disease, who knew we were about to arrest him, hung himself. The dead man was about to be added to the list of twenty-three former and current Buildings Department inspectors DOI arrested on a total of 264 counts of grand larceny through extortion and receiving unlawful gratuities. Under the arrangement these crooked inspectors had forced on plumbing contractors, the contractors routinely paid bribes ranging from

$50 to $1,000 to expedite the processing of required inspection reports so they could be paid for the job at hand and move on to the next one.

The Parkinson's-afflicted inspector, who know we had arrested the others—many of them at a training seminar we had asked the Buildings Department to call for that purpose—hung himself at home after coming to the correct conclusion that he was also on the list of potential arrestees. It's too bad no one was able to let him know that all we wanted out of arresting him was some information and that the charges against him would have been dropped on account of his physical condition.

BAILMAN SCAM

The sun penetrates into privies,
but is not polluted by them.—Diogenes

Shepard, like every other city bureaucrat, was always fighting to maintain or increase her department's budget. Unfortunately, under Dinkins, our budget was reduced four years in a row.

The indefatigable Shepard nevertheless kept telling other city officials how much we had saved the city by ending corrupt careers with arrests, a number that exceeded our budget. She'd point out that if an individual had been allowed to continue to steal, the city would have been out hundreds of thousands of dollars. She always underplayed these estimates rather than hype them. Nevertheless, even when presented conservatively, the figures involved were very impressive. So Shepard wasn't pleased one late spring day when she heard that a case we closed might actually cost the city half-a-million dollars rather than save it anything at all.

The crook in question was Arnold Terravecchia. One day he realized he was sitting on top of a big pile of money, and no one was watching him.

Terravecchia, a stout little man of forty-four, was also the official who collected the cash payments made by people who wanted to bail their friends and relatives out of one of the city's prisons. During the late 1980s, anyone paying bail to release an inmate from this major correctional facility would pay the money to Terravecchia, in cash. Terravecchia would put the money in a safe and give the payer a receipt. Then he'd collect money from the next person and the next.

The problem was that Terravecchia was the only person assigned to this duty at this particular prison. In a better-run world, someone else would have been around to make sure all copies of the receipts were kept on file and turned in along with the money. But this particular prison was hardly the epicenter of an ideal world, and Terravecchia was on his own. So whenever he needed some extra cash, he'd merely throw his copy of the receipt in the wastebasket and pocket the bail money.

He was able to get away with this ploy because the wheels of justice grind slowly. It was usually many months before a trial was held or a bargained guilty plea was entered and the person for whom bail had been paid was either sentenced to jail or freed from the clutches of the system. It was only then that Terravecchia was required to return the bail money that had been entrusted to him. And whenever he looked down, he saw $2 million a year passing through his hands.

At some point it occurred to him that he could take a free loan of a few hundred thousand dollars whenever he wished and no one would be the wiser. Since he liked to gamble—and was sure he'd make a killing one day—he didn't see anything wrong with borrowing the money, taking it to Atlantic City on his vacations, returning it safely, and keeping his winnings as profit.

Terravecchia wasn't a particularly good gambler, however, and he kept losing the money he took to the gambling spa. But he knew that if he failed to return the bail money to the people to whom it was due, he'd be caught.

All he was able to think of was to delay the people due bail until more cash came in the window, maybe later that day, maybe later that week, maybe later that month, and then give the new cash to the original payee as if he were actually returning it. This required delays, but everyone who dealt with the prison system was accustomed to them. After a while, however, Terravecchia was half-a-million dollars behind in his repayments.

A number of bail payers began complaining that they were waiting months for the return of their money. Their complaints reached DOI Inspector General Michael Caruso, a large man with a large belly, a thick Brooklyn accent, and a big mustache. A jovial fellow who was also a career civil servant, Caruso read every issue of the *Chief-Leader*, the civil-service newspaper, with the same dedication and concentration with which a professional handi-capper would read the *Racing Form*. He could quote civil-service test numbers for weeks after the issue came out. This sort of atten-tion to detail made Caruso a worthy opponent for Terravecchia.

Although Caruso wasn't a professional accountant, he and the investigators who worked for him took a look at Terravecchia's books after the complaints started coming in and noticed some-thing very strange. Whenever Terravecchia went on vacation and someone else took over his job, the books were balanced and the bail refunds paid promptly. When Terravecchia returned, the late payments and the long delays started again and the books resumed their lopsided course.

Caruso decided that a DOI accountant should go over the books. But the inspector general was no fool. Even he could see from his relatively inexpert look at the ledgers that Terravecchia was a fast man with a pencil and would quickly organize a cover-up if he had the chance. So Caruso had him transferred from his office at the jailhouse to an office at Correction Department head-quarters, not so coincidentally right next to Caruso's own.

With Terravecchia safely under Caruso's watchful eye, the DOI accountant went over the books and compared them to the receipts held by people whose bail money Terravecchia hadn't yet returned. He could come to only one conclusion. Terravecchia had taken the money and should be arrested. So Caruso arrested him. He then persuaded the district attorney to charge him with grand larceny, for which Terravecchia faced a fifteen-year maximum sentence. (He eventually was sentenced to eighteen to fifty-four months in prison.)

Terravecchia was probably relieved. They don't make loans at the prison commissary, so any gambling he might end up doing in jail would probably be for low stakes.

After Caruso alerted Correction Department officials to the problem, they split the responsibility for collecting and returning bail money among several employees, so no one working alone could think strange and wonderful thoughts about the cash piling up in front of him.

In spite of Caruso's work, it was DOI's ox that was gored. Once Terravecchia was arrested, his half-a-million dollar gambling debt had to be acknowledged and the corresponding gap in the city's bail accounts had to be filled with taxpayers' money. On paper at least, DOI had cost the city $500,000. Shepard was not pleased.

THE INCOMPLETE DOMINION OF MIDDLE-CLASS THINKING

*Like all fools, they believe themselves
safe from discovery.*
—Sir Francis Walshingham

DOI investigators waded in such a morass of everyday crooked-
ness that they were rarely surprised by any individual crime. In
fact, there were so many crimes being committed that after a
while the simple weight of so much crime seemed to create a
momentum that caused other crimes to be committed almost
involuntarily. As one DOI investigator said of the perps he

encountered, "They do wrong so long they begin to think it's right."

Addiction to money, rather than need for money, was a major factor. Some of the most flagrant and most successful crooks we encountered were also among the richest, the most established, and the most successful of people. And precisely because they were so rich and established and above suspicion, they stole millions through complex schemes that were often very difficult, or impossible, to penetrate. They believed their power would protect them from prosecution, and they were wrong.

But occasionally the agency's investigators would run across a crime that no one with the intelligence God gave geese could ever conceivably believe would not be detected. Now it's possible that the crooks in these cases needed the money desperately and knew that the penalties for a first-time offender were so low (often probation for low-level crimes) that they could safely scoop up what they needed knowing that when they were caught, they'd never do jail time.

There's another possible explanation. The incomplete dominion of middle-class thinking. A person who thinks middle class, and is not addicted to money, whether his or her income qualifies him officially as middle class or not, sees his life as a continuous progression stretching forward into the future and weighs risks accordingly. The middle-class person, even if he's dishonest, will contemplate the possibility of a crime and think about all he has to lose. Is it worth the risk? If he takes that $3,000 and is caught, is it worth risking a $45,000 job and having a picture of himself in handcuffs published in the paper for all his neighbors to cluck over?

But a non-middle-class type, regardless of race or religion, will think, "There's $300. I may not get caught. So why not take it?" and never calculate the risks. Nilsa De Los Santos, a former rent collector, illustrates this to a T.

Her story began when one privately owned building after another ran into trouble during the city's tough years in the early nineties. The owners of many of the buildings found themselves unable or unwilling to pay their property taxes. City authorities took control of these properties but allowed the tenants to remain as long as they continued to pay rent . . . to the city.

In some cases, the city allowed the tenants to form a tenants' association in each building or group of buildings. De Los Santos was elected treasurer of her building's association. One of her duties was collecting the rents and keeping records of her collections. Seeing her opportunity, she persuaded a number of tenants to give her money orders with the "Pay To" line left blank. She would then fill in her own name instead of the tenant association's.

Money orders were particularly attractive to people with goals like De Los Santos's because, although many people at least glance at the checks they write once the checks are returned by the bank, people who write money orders never see them again and have no idea in whose pockets they end up.

It's hard to believe that De Los Santos thought she could get away with the game she was playing for very long since a higher-up in the building's bureaucracy and another one in the city's bureaucracy knew what the building was supposed to be producing in rent. The fact is, she didn't. A higher-up questioned her about the missing money after she had accumulated about $9,000, and she confessed. A DOI audit of the apartment project's books then confirmed the details of her confession.

Although the $9,000 made this a penny-ante case—De Los Santos was eventually sentenced to three years probation—the DOI investigators involved were excited about it. Their excitement was due to the delicious possibility that De Los Santos wasn't worried about getting caught because her higher-ups were in on the game and she was paying them off. And maybe they were paying off their higher-ups. And maybe those higher-ups were paying off their higher-ups. Maybe . . .

Investigators drooled at the thought of arresting De Los Santos and telling her she'd go to jail unless she ratted on those above her, then doing the same thing at the next level . . . and the next.

In many cases, though, including De Los Santos's, one lone person would be nabbed, and the trail would lead no further. Either the person had no coconspirators at higher levels or wouldn't turn them in. The case would begin and end with the one low-level criminal.

De Los Santos was low level in another way as well—only limited guts were required to fill in one's own name on a blank money order. More boldness was required to try to cash a check on which someone else's name already had been written. In fact, a person who was supposed to be bold by occupation, one of the city's fire-fighters, tried this one day.

This fellow, Paul Gilliam, a firefighter on limited duty who worked at Fire Department headquarters, managed to get his hands on a couple of someone else's paychecks. Ironically enough, that someone was an employee of the city's massive Human Resources Administration, which issues many checks that are misused in fairly sophisticated ways. In this case, though, the HRA employee was robbed of the checks in a not-so-sophisticated way. Someone stuck a gun in his face and took them out of his pocket. No one was ever arrested for this crime, so we don't know how Gilliam got them. But we do know that Gilliam then forged the HRA employee's name on the back of the checks and took them to a check-cashing place.

Not too intelligently, Gilliam went to the same check-cashing place where he routinely cashed his own legitimate checks, which, of course, bore his own name. The check casher was surprised at the appearance of a new name on a check being handed in on behalf of a familiar face and inquired. Gilliam immediately fled, not helping his case any. His case wasn't helped much either when he left the checks behind, with the name of the real payee on front and his own attempt at forgery on the back. Not that it made much difference. He was handed three years on probation as a sentence.

Russell David was a bit trickier than Fireman Gilliam. David was the owner of a check-cashing store in the Bronx frequented by welfare recipients. The city paid the rent of many of these welfarites with two-party checks, made out both to the welfare recipient and to her landlord, and sent to the welfarite. The idea was that the welfarite would sign the check, then turn it over to her landlord, who would add his signature to the back of the check and deposit it in his own account. This system allowed both the tenant and landlord to know the rent had been paid and allowed the welfarite to withhold rent if services weren't provided.

But many welfare recipients could think of better things to do with these checks than pay their rent, especially when they knew that if the check never made it to the landlord, the city would in some cases pay it directly anyway. Buying baby shoes, buying drugs, buying liquor, buying extra food—a number of possibilities beckoned. But they all required cash, and this Russ David was willing to provide. If you brought him a two-party check made out to yourself and your landlord, he'd give you cash for it—something your landlord would never do—forge the landlord's endorsement on the back and deposit it in his own account. The allegedly ever-vigilant employees of the privately owned banks involved either never noticed or didn't care that neither of the two names on the check was David's or were paid not to notice. David managed to deposit 391 checks worth $80,000 in his own account over a couple of years. I hope he kept copies of the checks so he can study his handiwork during his five-year sentence.

CHECK OUT THE PAIN

People hated it when we hurt them. Not so much the people we arrested—they always seemed too stunned to feel anything. It was their agencies' public relations people who screamed the loudest when they took it on the chin.

I must admit that they sometimes had cause to. For obvious reasons, we couldn't tell them about an arrest of one of their coworkers until after the arrest had been made. But then, because publicity was the chief punishment and timeliness was necessary for maximum publicity, we had to get the relevant press release out fast. As I've said, Shepard wanted our releases to include a statement from the gored department, for fairness' sake.

But if the arrest took place at 10 A.M. and we wanted to put out the release—which I'd usually written the day before—at 11 A.M., we couldn't give the gored department's flack much time to work out his (or her) statement on the issue or to carefully word his commissioner's response. And I'd be constantly on his back, trying to wring that comment out of him so we could go ahead with our publicity barrage. Few of my fellow public-information people liked to get my call, but virtually everyone returned it. And the anger of my coworkers was my constant companion.

And hey, I could see their point. Not just about the short time we allotted them, but about the sequence of events from their point of view. Although it was true that a large percentage of our investigations were begun because of something we had discovered or had been tipped off about anonymously, tips about wrongdoing often came from officials or employees of the agency that we then proceeded to investigate. Because it took a while to find out who at the agency was involved in whatever plot we were probing, and because we wanted to tell as few people as possible what we were doing, we'd usually do the investigation without the active cooperation of the department.

Of course, when we arrested those involved, we'd announce it as a DOI investigation, which it was. But it seemed to the other department as if they were being punished for coming to us in the first place when, for instance, we'd arrest the second-in-command of the department as a result of a tip from the third-in-command. The public didn't often notice such fine differentiations. All they knew was—another scandal at the Transportation Department. My, my, my.

So I could understand the anger involved when an employee of the Borough of Manhattan Community College who had worked an entire six months in the college's mail room managed to make the whole college look bad by getting arrested by DOI.

BMCC was supported by the city. Specifically, that meant that the Finance Department sent checks to BMCC that the college then used to pay its bills. Checks for $10,000, $11,500, $12,000 floated lazily through the spring air of the BMCC mail room, handled somewhat resentfully by low-paid mail-room workers hungry for the luxuries of life.

One of these employees, Joyce Patterson, realized one day, after being on the payroll for only a few months, that there was just enough room above the words "Borough of Manhattan Community College" on the payee line of each check to type in her own name or the name of one of her friends. Since banks, being those wonderfully stable and responsible capitalist institutions that they are, exercise as much vigilance over their deposits as their cousins, the savings and loans, exercised over their loans before they collapsed, it would be easy, Patterson thought, to deposit these illegally altered and endorsed checks in her own or her friends' bank accounts. She figured her friends wouldn't mind her using their bank accounts, even if she eventually withdrew the money, if she let them keep some of the proceeds for their trouble.

She was right on all counts. After only a short while, she'd stolen, altered, deposited, and cashed checks worth $95,000.

Her crime was a pretty stupid one, considering the trail of evidence it left. What she hadn't realized was that the problem facing DOI's inspector generals in most of their cases wasn't discovering that a crime had been committed—we were surrounded with criminality—but in finding the evidence to prove who did it. Crimes backed by insufficient evidence to sustain a courtroom prosecution were as thick as the voluminous folders in DOI's harried Complaint Bureau.

But this case produced evidence that was hard to top. The check, with the perpetrators' names neatly typed on them and their real signatures on the back, were deposited by them in their own bank accounts, which they thoughtfully maintained in their real names. And, of course, the canceled checks were eventually collected and sent back to BMCC, the victim, where the inspector general on the case, Joe Gubbay, found them in the college's canceled-check files.

One of the conspirators, as if to help the energetic Gubbay wrap up the case even more quickly than he would have otherwise, went so far as to cash his altered BMCC check at a check-cashing establishment. There he was photographed automatically, thus adding his picture, attached to the stolen and illegally altered check he had cashed, to the growing pile of evidence.

The fact that the major player in this case, Patterson, had given the checks to numerous friends for deposit also helped. It enabled Gubbay to locate a lot of people who had cashed relatively small checks, arrest them, and threaten them with jail and disgrace unless they testified against those who had cashed the biggest checks.

But at least Patterson could be written off as a marginal figure at the college, a criminal so low as to be hidden from the view of almost every responsible academic official. Her sentence was pretty marginal, too—five years probation. The same could not be said about another city university employee, this one a Ph.D. candidate, who was arrested for waving a magic wand.

The inspector general involved in this case, Michael Caruso, usually made his arrests at the city's jails, as paradoxical as that might sound. He was an expert on those correctional institutions, and the 20,000 prisoners they held. He moved from one facility to another, day after day and night after night, collaring an inmate buying drugs here, a guard brutalizing a prisoner there, a medic smuggling guns to cons somewhere else.

In this case, though Caruso's arrestee wasn't a con or a correction officer but a mild-mannered City College employee, Ph.D. candidate and computer nerd, Fred Daniels. According to DOI, Daniels had persuaded college officials to let him take some of their computer equipment home, so he could work overtime for free (and surreptitiously add to the services he could offer through his private graphics business, which he ran out of his house). He also bought a laser wand to go with the computer equipment. This was a device that, once waved over something, would reproduce it to near perfection on the computer screen, from which it could then be altered and the altered version reprinted.

No one would have objected to Daniels waving his wand indefinitely except that what he chose to reproduce, according to the accusations against him, were Correction Department and Police Department parking permits that allowed their possessors to park in otherwise illegal parking spots. He would then insert someone's name in the appropriate place and print out what appeared to be legitimate permits on his $3,000 laser printer, Caruso and Shepard said.

Not only would these permits allow those who allegedly bought them from Daniels to park in spaces reserved for law-enforcement agents all over the city, they could also use them as fake police IDs for all sorts of nefarious purposes.

When Daniels and a customer disputed the price that had been paid for one of these made-to-order permits, according to Caruso, the customer decided he'd been cheated and called DOI. Caruso's subsequent appearance at Daniels's front door with a search warrant put an end to the Ph.D.'s alleged wand waving. But only a few of the phony permits were recovered.

In any case, Daniel's magic wand may have retained its power. The case against him has been sealed, precluding the release of any information on the disposition of the charges against him and on any sentence he may have received. It's possible he provided state's evidence on another case.

COOKING THE BOOKS: CORRUPTION AT THE LIBRARY

It was relatively easy to get the taxpayers and the reporters who ostensibly represented them to believe that welfare recipients were stealing millions of taxpayer dollars. Welfare cheats were right up there with building inspectors and parking-meter coin collectors as believable DOI arrestees. What was difficult to persuade reporters and the public was that the little old ladies at the public library were greasing their palms with illicit loot. But they were.

And cigars, Liz Holtzman, political paybacks, and some amazing long-term stonewalling were heavily involved.

It all began with an anonymous tipster, probably an employee of the Queens Borough Public Library who was about to be laid off. The informant told DOI that library administrators were giving themselves large salary increases, taking luxurious trips and vacations, buying new cars, and treating themselves to lavish banquets with the millions of dollars the library's clerks collected from the thousands of five-cent-a-day fees charged patrons for overdue books. This was at a time when library service was being reduced from five to four days a week, with hundreds of employees being laid off, to save the library money.

The old DOI, in its unaggressive way, referred the letter to the office of City Comptroller Elizabeth Holtzman, on the grounds that a 1907—yes, a 1907—agreement between the city and the library authorized the comptroller to conduct annual audits of the library.

The library had such a clean smell about it, the comptroller was a bit behind on her audit schedule. As of 1990, eighty-three years after the signing of the agreement, neither the comptroller nor anyone else had ever audited the library, a $42-million-a-year institution.

Holtzman was aggressive enough, however, to use the note as a reason for ordering her aides to conduct the first-ever audit of the library. Its officials were quite willing to allow Holtzman's people to audit the 80 percent of its funding the library received from the city, but refused to allow them to even glance at the 20 percent it received from the federal and state governments, from corporate sponsors and private individuals, and from overdue book fines.

This denial was clearly contrary to the 1907 agreement and illegal. But Liz, who had called for the impeachment of the president of the United States when she had served in Congress, backed down when confronted by the steely-eyed librarians, their attorneys, and their political backers. She decided not to subpoena the records the library refused to reveal, even though her public responsibilities demanded she do so. Then, after finding nothing amiss with the records the librarians allowed her to audit, she notified Shepard that that was the end of the investigation as far as the comptroller was concerned.

Shepard was not the type to be denied. She sent a DOI investigator to ask for the same records Holtzman had been refused. When library officials once again refused, Shepard, rather than backing off, subpoenaed the records.

The librarians, apparently unacquainted with Shepard's mood when she was denied something she wanted, moved to quash the subpoena in court. Now even more determined to overcome the reluctance of some public officials to allow other public officials to look at the expenditure records of a public institution, Shepard refused to back off. In fact, she did the opposite, sending Bob Brackman, the DOI's hard-working deputy commissioner for investigations and a hard-fisted prosecutor if ever there was one, to argue for the subpoena in court.

As Brackman knocked down one argument after another put forward by the library's socially prominent attorney, Anthony H. Atlas, and the judge's comments indicated the decision would go DOI's way, the librarians began to realize that "Library Resists Investigators; Financial Records Suspect; Court Orders Documents Revealed" wasn't the sort of publicity they wanted. They caved, sending Shepard the records.

It soon became apparent why the library didn't want DOI studying their accounts. This was a time when some branches were open for only three days a week and many others were closed on the weekends. Low-paid library employees were being laid off by the score. Library officials were threatening to close twenty-five branches. And yet, the members of the library's board of trustees had during one twelve-month period spent $800 on cigars, $17,000 for meals, $63,000 on travel and conferences, and thousands to buy tickets to political fund-raisers. Larger amounts were spent on "salary enhancements" and benefit plans. More money was spent on politically well-connected consultants.

Two hundred thousand dollars was spent between 1987 and 1992 buying tickets for trustees to attend such events as the annual Boy Scouts Dinner, the Queens Federation of Churches festival, and Pride of Judea Mental Health banquets. The librarians justified these tickets by insisting that they would result in future contributions to the library from these groups. But the reality was that only about a third of the amount the library had spent had been returned in the form of such contributions. Insiders said the real reason for the library's charitable largesse was to get in good with prominent Queens politicians such as Borough President Claire Shulman and Council Speaker Peter Vallone, who supported all those groups and who loved to see other groups or institutions contribute to their favorites.

In fact, the library spent more than $1 million a year on "inappropriate items," in DOI's words. And it had been doing so, as far as anyone could tell, since 1907. Furthermore, the library was accumulating money much faster than it could spend it and had not made the slightest move to apply any of the excess to the actual expenses of the library.

It's not difficult to predict the reaction of a library patron who paid a fifty-cent fine on an overdue library book or stood in line for change so he could put three dollars in dimes into the copying machine if he knew the money he had just given to the clerk had gone to purchase a cigar for a trustee. But from an accountant's point of view, the situation was even worse. For as many as eighty-three years, the library had been depositing the money it had received from the city in interest-paying accounts and using the interest for its cigars, meals, and political contributions. By 1990, the Queens Public Library had $13 million it could draw on for these purposes.

DOI officials wondered why the mayor's Office of Management and Budget hadn't taken this money into account when squeezing money out of the highly overstrained public treasury to support library operations. OMB responded that taking such funds into account would discourage the library from seeking charitable contributions. This was an odd explanation since charitable contributions weren't kept in the account in which DOI had found the problems.

Eventually OMB agreed to consider the library's $13-million fund when distributing library appropriations the next year. A *New York Newsday* reporter wrote a couple of stories on the fund. But no one else picked up the story, and I never could get anyone excited about the fact that the money painstakingly inserted in copying machines at libraries and handed over in the form of fines for tattered overdue books . . . went for luxuries.

In late 1996, Holtzman's successor, Alan Hevesi, taking his cue from Shepard, once again asked the Queens Borough Public Library for its complete financial records. The library refused.

DOI ARRESTS DOI

Who guards the guards?—Juvenal

You'd think a DOI investigator would have known better. Okay, okay, all he did was work in the background unit, which means what he did for seven years was investigate people who had applied for jobs with city agencies. But still, after watching other investigators dragging manacled perps down the halls and after listening to other investigators boast about the complex cases they'd cracked, you'd think he'd know enough not to leave DOI for another city department and then, allegedly, put his hand in the till, opening himself up to arrest . . . by DOI.

But that's exactly what he did. And when we arrested him, we did it in the full glare of publicity, with me, Mr. Flack, standing there with egg on my face while current DOI agents arrested a former DOI agent and newspaper photographers took pictures of investigators clamping handcuffs on our former comrade.

It reminded me of the England of a few hundred years ago, when pickpockets were hung before huge crowds of spectators to deter other pickpockets from continuing their criminal careers. While spectators craned their necks and became hypnotized by the sight of strangling men swinging in the breeze, their pockets would be picked by other pickpockets, who were too busy stealing to pay any attention to the supposed deterrents turning purple just above their heads.

Of course, it's possible that this investigator, Fred Anders, had a slightly different reaction. Once he saw how many crimes people were committing that DOI never got to, he may have figured that his $26,000 annual salary wasn't so princely and that he could earn more by switching sides. He took a city job emptying parking meters.

Taxes aside, autos—parking them, fining them, towing them, storing them—were where the money was. Anders soon realized he had stepped into a honey pot.

The city had been trying for decades to keep whoever was collecting parking money from stealing some of it from New York's 63,000 parking meters. Workers employed by a private contractor had collected from the meters for years, until the early 1990s, but stole so efficiently and were arrested in such vast numbers that municipal officials decided to give city workers a try.

They coupled the new forty-eight-member workforce with new technology. The coins inserted in each meter would drop straight into a locked coin box. The collectors were equipped with a sort of keg on wheels with a hole on top, which they pulled behind them. Their job was to remove the unopenable coin box from the meter, stick its neck into the hole in the keg, and turn it sharply. The quarters would empty directly into the keg, which was also unopenable. Then the collectors would truck the kegs back to headquarters.

This system, into which millions was poured for the design and production of coin boxes and kegs, worked very well for about an hour. Then it collapsed. It ran head on into the desperation of city drivers intent on finding a place to park, even if they had to feed silver to a meter to stay in that parking place. In addition, there was the desire of approximately two-thirds of the collectors to supplement the $16,000 a year the city was paying them, by illegal means if necessary.

Sometimes these two factors worked hand in hand. Drivers would slip quarters into the meters day and night, rain or shine, twenty-four hours a day if necessary, but there was no way the collectors could empty every meter every day. That meant the coin box in many meters often overflowed. Quarters inserted in the meter bounced off the top of the box and fell down into the tube holding it, or piled up on top of the box. The collectors, instead of grabbing on to a smooth coin box when they opened a meter, would find their hands buried in a pile of shiny quarters. Who could resist such a windfall? About one-third of the collectors, that's who. (The dishonest collectors called the honest ones "the holies.")

The other two-thirds, not to be overly obvious about it, wore coats or shirts with big pockets, or gloves with big wristbands, and stashed away quarters in these handy interstices. (Some collectors even wore the heavy gloves in combination with their summer T-shirts, so their stealing could continue year round.) Collectors with small hands did best at this sort of work. They could get those very last quarters at the bottom of each meter housing even while wearing gloves. The fifty or so tax-free dollars the collectors could slip out of the meters in this way each day came in handy.

Sometimes the collectors helped this process along, paradoxically, by not collecting anything at all from every other meter on their route. This would double the overflow quarters for the next collector. It also showed what a complex and interconnected culture of criminality could be nurtured in city soil, because, in anticipation of something like this happening, meter officials had never allowed the same collectors to collect from the same group of meters two days in a row. They could see no reason the noncollecting collectors would want to enrich their colleagues who would visit the meters the next day by not collecting from the meters every day.

But this antitheft plan failed. The collectors still didn't collect from those meters every day, not because they were altruistic but because they were secure in the knowledge that since two-thirds of the department was criminal, the favor would be returned on their new route the next day or the day after.

And, of course, they didn't stop there. If it was the coin boxes that were getting in their way, hey, get rid of the coin boxes! A crooked collector would remove the coin box, empty it into the keg and then throw it away. That meant that the next time he or a fellow crooked collector came back to that meter, they could purloin all the coins rather than just some of them, usually netting about $600 worth of quarters. Soon the city was littered with coin boxes.

Occasionally, those citizens sharp enough to recognize a discarded coin box as something that came out of a parking meter would call DOI or the Transportation Department and report that they had found what they presumed was a searched-for item, rather than a discarded one. Due to these calls, and the efforts of the honest collectors, most of the coin boxes were replaced within a few days, but not before the jacket pockets of the crooked collectors had grown even fatter.

This flaw in the system was not necessarily foreseeable, but others certainly were. The key, for instance. One key opened all the coin boxes in the city. No one should have been surprised, then, that within a few days it was conveniently "lost" and had to be replaced. This meant two keys were in the system, one for the honest collectors and one for the dishonest ones.

The man who had stolen the key and who jealously kept possession of it soon became top dog in the department. He also became enormously fat and stood out, because of his girth, in a workplace culture of thin muscular men and women. He was fat because he was living what was from his point of view a near-ideal life. Sure he had to come to work . . . he had the key. But from then on, it was fat city. He'd start the day by guzzling gallons of orange juice and milk and inhaling stacks of syrup-drenched pancakes. Then, his stomach swollen, he would fall asleep in the back of the collectors' van while others did his collecting for him. He'd wake only to take his cut from the flow of quarters the key produced before calling it a day and going home tired, happy, and several pounds heavier.

This was hardly a usual day for a city employee, but this ring within a ring, called the "key club," did imitate at least one city employment practice. It made allowances for absences. A key club member who was home sick would lose neither his licit or his illicit income. His legal salary would continue due to city-authorized sick pay, and his illicit take would continue because, by pre-arrangement, his colleagues would hold his share and give it to him on his return.

Although fat, the king of the key club was not crude. After all, he used a key. Some of his cohorts, however, didn't even attempt to imitate his rather gentlemanly standards. They used brute force where he had used his brain. Deprived of possession of the key, these men would take the poor coin boxes into their vans and beat them to death with crowbars or shovels. They'd then pocket the quarters and discard the bent and broken boxes.

These larcenous activities were so successful that the thieves soon faced a new problem—what to do with all the quarters they were filching. Some tried the direct approach. One collector bought a couple of bottles of perfume with $80 worth of quarters. But this would hardly do for purchasing automobiles, for instance. It wasn't long before, like other entrepreneurs, they sought out those people in society who needed their product and marketed the product directly to them. In this case, it was merchants who needed quarters for their daily business and who had to pay a quarter for each roll they purchased from a bank. The collectors charged nothing for their quarters, and the banks were soon out of the picture.

Within a short while, produce scales were being used to weigh stacks of quarters, fresh from the parking meters, for which the merchants would pay in $5, $10, and $20 bills. Some merchants were so anxious for their quarters fix, they'd run out into their parking lots when the collectors' vehicles pulled in, yelling "Do you have quarters for me today?"

The flow of stolen coins was so vast—DOI investigators eventually averaged it out at four million quarters per year—that, inevitably, not all of them could be disposed of on the day of collection. Some had to be loaded into sacks and dropped off at the collectors' apartments before they drove their vans back to the department to sign out. The quarters then had to be inserted in paper rolls and taken to the bank. But hey, somebody had to do it.

It was into this world that former Investigator Anders, now pushing sixty-five, transferred a short while after leaving DOI, a world of clinking quarters and comradely laughter.

What he didn't know was that he was followed into the ranks of the collectors a few months later by a DOI undercover agent.

But before resorting to the drawn-out and expensive task of inserting an agent, DOI investigators had attempted to crack the ring using more conventional methods. First they installed cameras in what appeared to be grocery or milk trucks to film the collectors as they stole, but immediately ran into a recognition problem. Traffic enforcement agents, enemies of the department, pointed out the DOI vans to the parking-meter collectors, who would mug cooperatively for the cameras. Not that this stopped them from stealing. Once they knew where the van was, they could position themselves between the camera and the meters so their stealing could not be taped. This, of course, made their thievery less efficient, but it also prevented the gathering of any taped evidence.

All that remained, therefore, was the undercover. Having been placed in the department, he ran into some bureaucratic delays and then into a natural delay—summer. His handlers thought his evidence would stand up in court only if he wore a wire, but the clothes the collectors wore in hot weather were too scanty to conceal the necessary equipment. Finally, though, fall rolled around, heavier clothes were called for, and the gathering of recorded evidence began.

After six months, the case was ready. Ellen Kay Schwartz, a DOI inspector general who enjoyed dressing flamboyantly for early-morning arrests, was polishing her red cowboy boots in preparation for her big day at collector headquarters. But word of the planned raid leaked out, and David Seifman, city hall bureau chief of the *New York Post*, the most flamboyant of the city's newspapers, called to tell me that he knew the raid was planned and that he was going to write about it in advance unless we gave him a good reason not to.

This was one of the very few occasions on which Shepard caved when confronted by press pressure. She did it to protect the undercover. On many other occasions, other reporters, exercising their bluffing muscles, had called to tell me that they *knew*

DOI was investigating so-and-so, so why didn't I just tell them about it? Following Shepard's guidelines, my usual response was "If you really know about it, and I'm not saying there's any 'it,' then write your story. Why do you need us to say anything?" Usually no story resulted. Seifman rarely, if ever, attempted that particular trick. We were forced to assume he really knew enough to write this story. And because our undercover was still on the job, we couldn't take the chance that if we blew Seifman off, he wouldn't call our bluff.

The situation was stickier for us than Seifman realized because the undercover could not be withdrawn in time to avoid the story and still keep the investigation intact. And if the crooked collectors guessed the undercover's identity, he might well be in big trouble.

That was partly because the collectors, unlike many of the other city employees we arrested, needed very few skills to obtain their jobs. The only two requirements were a driver's license and an ability to lift a seventy-pound bag (presumably full of quarters). A large number of people had both these qualifications, including some who carried guns, some who used cocaine, some who engaged in criminal enterprises on the side, and some who did all three, making them more prone to violence than the insurance-clerk types with whom we often dealt.

So we made a deal with Seifman. We'd let a *Post* reporter and photographer along on the raid if the *Post* promised not to write about the raid until after it happened.

Both sides kept to their agreement, and there I was, early in the morning at collector headquarters, standing on a loading dock while the inspector general's boots blazed in the light of early dawn, and DOI investigators patted down one collector after another, arresting each of the twenty culprits in turn.

Anders, late to work that day, pulled up at the loading dock amidst the unmistakable hallmarks of a DOI raid—the handcuffs, the uniforms, the twenty sedans, the sixty investigators, and the unusual but telling *Post* photographer's flashgun popping away. Several DOI investigators handcuffed their former colleague, shaking their heads.

Charges against four of the collectors were conditionally discharged. Two were wrist-slapped with five-year probations. And five were sentenced to terms ranging from four months to one year in jail each. Anders's case was sealed. His sentence, if any, remains unknown.

GINGER MAN

God's mercy on the wild
Ginger Man!—J. P. Donleavy

The Ginger Man case dramatically demonstrated Shepard's lust for an independent DOI. Political influence, high officialdom, and the arrogance of being "in" were all clearly manifested in Ginger Man, as well as DOI's determination to stamp out such privileges.

The Ginger Man was a restaurant in the Lincoln Center area owned by Dinkins supporter Mike O'Neal and his brother, actor Patrick O'Neal, who had played the title character in the Broadway run of the play *The Ginger Man*. Mayor Dinkins, two deputy mayors, and the city attorney often ate at the Ginger Man restaurant.

The restaurant's connection with DOI began when the Department of Health got tired of restaurants ignoring fines they'd been ordered to pay for various disgusting health-code violations. It issued an ultimatum to all eleven hundred or so establishments that hadn't paid up warning they had until a certain date to make good or they'd be closed down.

Some restaurants paid up. Being closed down isn't good for business, and the memory of those "Closed by the Health Department" signs on a restaurant's windows doesn't exactly encourage return business. Everyone knows what it takes to get a city bureaucracy moving. To actually close a place down, it's got to be filthy.

The Ginger Man, however, didn't pay in time. The Health Department, true to its word, posted notices in the restaurant's windows ordering it closed. But Mike O'Neal defied the order and stayed open. Business was too good for him to close that night, he told a Health Department official.

Health inspectors visited the restaurant the next morning, and finding five health-code violations on the premises, again ordered it closed. This time it complied. After all, it was still morning and the Ginger Man was primarily a dinnertime establishment. In any case, O'Neal immediately called his political friends and asked them for help in reopening before the supper hour.

Those friends—including Ken Sunshine, special executive assistant to the mayor—allegedly put pressure on the relevant Health Department officials, who felt compelled to allow the restaurant to reopen without forcing it to correct the code violations.

When inspectors visited the restaurant again six months later, as a matter of routine, they found "food stored at improper temperatures, cracked eggs, vermin activity likely to result in food contamination and an unprotected sewer pipe dripping in a food preparation area in the cellar."

According to the inspectors, when they expressed concern about the situation, O'Neal told them congenially to write down any violations they chose because he had connections and they wouldn't be able to close him down.

Once Sunshine heard that the Health inspectors had been bothering O'Neal again, things got worse. Having seen the Health Department yield to initial political pressure, he decided to extend city hall's reach. Sunshine told the Health Department to send him a list of restaurants it proposed to close before it closed them, apparently so he could veto any scheduled shutdowns if the restaurants were owned by people who had been or might become Dinkins campaign contributors.

Some Health inspectors complained to DOI. Shepard, even after learning who owned what and who was connected to whom, assigned an investigative team to the matter. The team wrote a report detailing the story above. Shepard immediately sent it to the mayor's office and the Health Department. Officials at both read the report, rolled their eyes heavenward, then stuck the report in a desk drawer. Shepard thought releasing it and punishing the guilty was not only the right thing to do but would boost the morale of both DOI and the restaurant inspectors, even though it certainly wouldn't help morale in the mayor's office or at his campaign committee headquarters.

So she was pleased when *New York Newsday* reporter Joe Calderone, after hearing rumors about the existence of such a report, sent in a Freedom-of-Information request for it. Such requests require the government bureaucracies to which they're addressed to release the documents requested, unless such release is exempted by law. The Ginger Man report was not exempt. We sent it to Calderone, who began writing what would have been a major Sunday exclusive, rich with quotes from the report and reaction from the mayor's friends and enemies.

First Deputy Mayor Norman Steisel heard of the report's release and screamed bloody murder at Shepard. She told him it was the department's duty to prepare the report and that the Freedom of Information Act tied her hands as far as releasing it was concerned. But Lee Jones, the mayor's press secretary, also learned of the impending bombshell and decided to strike first.

Sunday is the major circulation day for most newspapers. Not only do more people buy more newspapers on that day than any other, but they spend more time reading them as well. Sunday is also the day on which opinions about newspapers are formed, leading to purchases of daily papers later in the week. Readers sometimes even purchase Monday papers to follow a series that started on Sunday. A reporter scoring a Sunday exclusive will become a hero for at least a couple of days. That, of course, was Calderone's major goal.

By contrast, Saturday is death in the news business. The papers are small, and few are purchased. Many people spend Saturday doing chores and don't bother with the papers. If a public relations person wants to highlight a story, he holds a Saturday press conference aimed at the Sunday papers. If he wants to bury a story, he releases it Friday evening so the reporters will be forced by the pressure of competition to write it for Saturday, griping all the while about losing their Friday nights out and being forced to write for the minuscule Saturday audience.

For obvious reasons, Jones wanted the story buried. So, after DOI released the Ginger Man report to Calderone, while Calderone was still writing his Sunday story in the belief he was the only possessor of the report, Jones released copies to all the other reporters Friday afternoon. This left them no choice but to write it for Saturday. When Calderone realized what had been done, he had to write his story for Saturday as well or appear to be one day behind come Sunday.

Calderone was furious at losing his exclusive. His editors were also pissed off. A few weeks later, Schools Chancellor Joseph Fernandez offhandedly called Jones a "jerk" over some unrelated issue. None of the other papers ran a story on this rather minor remark, but *Newsday* played it near the front of the paper with accompanying photographs of Fernandez and Jones.

Although Jones had managed to blunt the political impact of the story, the report itself still fell heavily on the guilty. The Ginger Man closed, filed for bankruptcy, and reopened later in the same area under another name. Sunshine, the mayoral aide involved had already resigned. The Health Department official who had allowed the restaurant to remain open with violations was suspended for two weeks without pay. And DOI had slipped into the public consciousness, for the first time in years, as an agency that would write and release a blistering report about people at the highest levels of the administration that funded it.

DOI AND ELIZABETH HOLTZMAN: INSIDE THE POWER OF PUBLICITY

The corruption of the best is the worst.
—St. Thomas Aquinas

It all began with a press release from the mayor's office announcing that Mayor Dinkins and Comptroller Elizabeth Holtzman had decided which private firms would sell city bonds that year. The release actually announced that Dinkins and Holtzman had selected "seven financial services companies to serve as senior managers of the city's general obligation bond issues [new money and refundings] and any negotiated note issue." This seemingly mundane announcement was to plunge Holtzman into a political hurricane.

DOI and its publicity machine was at the eye of the storm and was, in fact, the reason for Holtzman's political demise. The old DOI would have quietly acquiesced in her attempt to put one over on the public. At several crucial points in the Holtzman saga, however, the new DOI had a choice and always came down on the side of stringent ethics rather than on Holtzman's side, even though she was the mayor's ally.

The mayor's press release created no excitement at first. After all, the city borrows money every year by selling bonds. Since bond selling is a specialized trade, and involves vast specialized knowledge, contacts, and finesse, it's best handled by the professionals who sell bonds for private companies on a daily basis. The list of firms selected to handle the city's bond sales that year was news in the trade press but big news in no other paper.

Then, something happened, and the spark that kindled the whole flammable mixture was—someone was pissed off. And not only was that person pissed off, but he or she decided to do something about it.

The annoying part of the press release from that person's point of view was its first few paragraphs, listing which big firms would get the most city bonds to sell and be paid the most for doing so. Naturally, this group included the usual Wall Street suspects. The big shock (to somebody) appeared in the sixth paragraph, in which Dinkins and Holtzman announced the firms being awarded the second largest number of bonds to sell. Included among the twenty-two firms in this category was Fleet Securities. The catch was that in the previous year, Fleet had been a member of a larger group of firms that had received a much smaller number of securities to sell.

Someone in the financial community read this, or heard about it, and became very angry. I strongly suspect it was someone who hated Holtzman's guts and who worked or had worked at Fleet Bank, which, as the name implies, was linked with Fleet Securities. Or perhaps it was a dismissed Holtzman employee. (A word to the wise—want to be safe? Don't ever fire, divorce, or piss off anyone.) What this person did was call either reporter Charles Gasparino at *The Bond Buyer* or reporter Jim McKinley at the *New York Times* and tell either or both of them that the reason Fleet had risen from the third group to the second was because it had loaned Holtzman a quick $450,000 just when she needed it. (Holtzman hadn't noted the loan in her official campaign reports.)

Holtzman had needed $450,000 in late August 1992 because her longtime ambition to be a United States senator was on the verge of being thwarted. She had kept her eyes on a Senate seat for decades. She'd started her career in the House of Representatives, where she was assigned to the House Judiciary Committee, not often the center of Washington action. But due to another source talking to another newspaper, the matter of the prospective impeachment of President Nixon came before the committee. Holtzman, never shy to begin with, seized the moment. Even though she was the youngest member of the committee in a House built on the dignity of age, she demanded President Nixon's impeachment in clear, ringing tones which were broadcast, along with her earnest face, on national television.

Nixon resigned shortly thereafter. Holtzman attempted to build on the popularity she had developed in the struggle against him by lunging for the gold ring—a U.S. Senate seat—in 1980. She was edged out by wily Alfonse D'Amato, a Republican who to this day remains the junior senator from New York.

From then on, Holtzman's only desire was to take on D'Amato again. But she had to maintain a presence in the public eye during the long years before D'Amato might again be vulnerable. So she ran for Brooklyn district attorney in 1981 and won. After she had completed her second term as D.A., she ran for city

comptroller, in 1989, and won. She wasn't overwhelmingly qualified for either job, but she was a widely known liberal crusader
and a smart politician with apparently unshakable integrity. She
was also, in an age and a region of growing feminism, a feminist.

When D'Amato came up for reelection again, in 1992, Holtzman, jumping at the chance of opposing him for a second time,
ran for the Democratic nomination for his seat. Joining her were
several other Democrats, including State Attorney General Robert
Abrams and community activist Al Sharpton. But this time,
another widely known woman also entered the lists: Geraldine Ferraro, the first woman ever nominated as the vice-presidential candidate of a major party. If Ferraro had not entered the senatorial
primary, Holtzman probably could have beaten Abrams, who
would have lost most of the female vote to Holtzman the feminist, and Sharpton, who would have lost much of the black vote
to Holtzman the liberal crusader.

But Ferraro had entered and stood directly in Holtzman's way.
Warm and motherly, but also skilled, intelligent, energetic, and
popular, Ferraro would clearly split the female and liberal vote
with Holtzman and doom Holtzman's candidacy.

Holtzman wasn't the type of person to sit around for another
few years waiting for a third chance for the Senate. She cam-
paigned hard against all three of her opponents. But it didn't work.
The polls showed her third in the race by late August, leading only
Sharpton. So she decided on a desperation move. She'd destroy
Ferraro, her major opponent, by linking Ferraro with organized
crime in a blast of last-minute TV spots, even though the evidence
for this charge—some raw data someone had filched from a police
file—was shaky. But by the time she made the decision to try this
last-minute offensive, she had spent all her campaign money and
was told the effort she planned against Ferraro would cost
$450,000. She borrowed the money from Fleet Bank, an institu-
tion that was hoping for more city bond business to come its way.

It was a wasted loan and a wasted effort. The attack commercials alienated everyone in sight, and Holtzman, with lots of name recognition and no stains on her record except those commercials, finished fourth—fourth!— in a four-person race, behind even Sharpton. Sharpton had never received the nomination of a major party for any office, had never held any office, and was seen by many as a mountebank and rabble-rouser. It was his statesmanlike demeanor on TV, while Holtzman cast looks of hatred at Ferraro, that allowed him to move from his expected fourth place to an unexpected and respectable third, behind only Abrams, the serving attorney general, and Ferraro, the former vice-presidential candidate, and ahead of the now widely disliked Holtzman.

Devastated, Holtzman didn't know what to do next. Nonetheless, she was still comptroller, the city's chief financial officer. While she tried to plan out her future, she decided to hold onto her job. It meant she'd have to run in the 1993 city primary election for renomination as the Democratic candidate for the office, after failing, in the 1992 election, to be nominated as the party's candidate for senator, but the odds were hardly insuperable.

One of her opponents was Alan Hevesi, a state assemblyman whose name-recognition factor was so low he called *himself* "Alan Who?" Her other opponent was Herman Badillo, who Mayor Koch had called "incompetent" and had dismissed as deputy mayor years before. Badillo, who wasn't even all that popular in the Latino community, had been out of public office for ten years and had failed in his various attempts to corral the Democratic mayoral nomination.

While it was true that Ferraro and many other prominent female politicians hated Holtzman for, as they saw it, torpedoing Ferraro's bid for the Senate, no one expected this resentment to propel Hevesi, the unknown assemblyman, or Badillo, the middle-aged accountant, to the top of the heap.

So Holtzman's campaign moved ahead without major difficulty until someone made the calls to Gasparino and McKinley. McKinley's story in the *Times* had the most immediate impact, of course. But both stories revealed the loan and implied that the quid pro quo for it was the substantial extra bond business Holtzman apparently had arranged for Fleet. Holtzman defended herself by saying that her staff had selected Fleet, not she, so the loan wasn't a conflict of interest. Alan Who? tried to make the charge stick, but since no one had ever heard of him, his effort didn't make much headway.

Holtzman, however, had not reckoned with the city's Conflicts of Interest Board. The mission of this very small city agency was, in part, to determine when the outside interests of a city official conflicted with his or her job and to order an offending official to stop ongoing behavior or penalize him or her for past behavior.

Since the board was assigned no investigators, the city charter gave it the power to assign investigations it wanted performed to DOI. After reading the McKinley-Gasparino revelations, a majority of board members asked DOI to determine if there was any conflict of interest in Fleet having lent Holtzman the money.

———

Since all communications between the COIB and DOI were secret under the charter, COIB's assigning of this investigation to DOI might not have made any difference one way or the other had not phones rung again on the desks of various reporters. This time it was other anti-Holtzmanites telling reporters that DOI was investigating her. Stories from unnamed sources about the DOI investigation began to appear in the papers.

Holtzman should have kept her mouth shut at this point, since she knew the COIB, and DOI under Shepard would never admit to conducting an investigation. Under previous administrations,

DOI might have told reporters off the record about the Holtz-man investigation, since the papers already knew about it. For the small price of telling some reporters what they already knew, the department might have gained some goodwill it could use later on.

Shepard was nothing, however, if not the Queen of Straight. We weren't supposed to tell reporters about ongoing investiga-tions, so we didn't. I had an electronic parrot in my office which could imitate me saying, "We can neither confirm nor deny that we're investigating any person or entity," when reporters called asking about current investigations. I occasionally daydreamed that if I could restrict those calls to one or two days a week, I could spend those days at the beach and leave the parrot in charge.

Holtzman, however, may not have realized how straight Shep-ard was. And, more importantly, the continued stories about the rumored DOI investigation were drying up her funding sources. She decided to eliminate the problem by asking the mayor to reconsider the joint decision the two of them had made to give Fleet the extra bond business. Given this opening by a political ally, Dinkins quickly decided that Fleet shouldn't be awarded the business. This meant there would be no practical result of Holtz-man's alleged misdeed. All and sundry would now assume, Holtz-man hoped, that the city was no longer being damaged by the matter, whoever was at fault, and would no longer concern them-selves with it.

Then, in attempt to administer the coup de grâce to the entire controversy, Holtzman herself announced, on May 7, that DOI was investigating the loan, hoping her statement would throw a soporific blanket over the entire affair. She could answer any ques-tions about the matter by saying she was completely innocent, that DOI was looking into it with her full cooperation, and that she could no longer answer any questions about, or comment on, the matter since interfering with a DOI investigation was a crime.

How dare the reporter ask her to violate a public trust by speaking out and breaking the law blah blah blah.

During DOI's years as an in-house puppet, Holtzman's coup de grâce would have succeeded. After all, Holtzman was an ally of the mayor and the mayor's appointee, Shepard, ran DOI. The entire affair would have been only a minor issue until maybe a year or two after the election, when DOI would have sent a namby-pamby report about it to the Conflicts of Interest Board. The board would have taken another two years to decide if Holtzman had been in a conflict-of-interest situation, and by then almost everyone would have forgotten what all the fuss was about in the first place.

Holtzman, however, did not count on Shepard's independence and drive. Shepard immediately assigned a team of top DOI lawyers to work on the investigation, put a very high DOI official in immediate command of the investigative team, and gave the team's work top priority. The investigators immediately requested papers and documents from Holtzman's office. Holtzman, obviously stalling, sent the required documents over in dribs and drabs, hoping the whole thing would blow over as planned. She maintained her lead in the polls as election day neared.

Not realizing how fast DOI was working with the documents it could wring out of Holtzman or how slowly Holtzman was supplying them to DOI, several newspaper editorialists and, of course, Holtzman's opponents in the race for comptroller, urged her publicly to pressure DOI to finish its investigation before the September 14 primary. Then the voters could decide whether she had been right or wrong in the Fleet matter before they went to the polls. Applying such pressure to the people investigating her was as far from Holtzman's mind as playing tennis on the moon.

Shepard had already decided to have the report completed before the primary just in case, but thought her own determination somewhat irrelevant since the report would not be made public before it was sent to the Conflicts of Interest Board. Once there, it would be examined by the board in confidence until long after the primary and general election were over. (Shepard's assumption was partly correct. It wasn't until April 1996 that the board said anything at all about the matter, when it fined Holtzman $7,500 for her actions in 1992 and 1993.)

Then Jack Newfield struck. The popular *New York Post* columnist, who had played a large part in the Parking Violations Bureau scandal that had ruined Mayor Koch a few years before, wrote a vitriolic piece denouncing DOI for not finishing and releasing the report before the primary. He wrote it while Shepard, her second-in-command, Richard Daddario, and I were all on vacation. His column began by implicitly denouncing each of us in turn for being away when we could be back in our offices pushing for the completion of the report. It ended by urging us to complete it and release it before the primary. The column was headlined, ET-style, "Susan Shepard—Call Home."

Holtzman's two opponents in the election leapt at the opportunity this presented. Badillo arranged a press conference in front of the DOI building at which he harangued a crowd of reporters and puzzled passers-by about how shameful it was for DOI not to release the report before the primary.

A scene from the musical *Best Little Whorehouse in Texas* was now reenacted outside DOI headquarters. In the scene, the governor of Texas appears at a press conference in which the nasty questions he's asked are represented by little arrows of light that fly toward him. Dressed in a dark suit, with a line of thirty male dancers behind him mimicking him in dress, words, and dance steps, he avoids each arrow, all the while singing "I like to do a little side step . . . "

Back from vacation, I was sent down to join Badillo's press conference in imitation of this tactic. As the rain began spattering the assembled TV cameras, I announced that DOI would have the report completed and sent to the COIB before the primary, but since the charter forbade us from releasing it, Badillo would have to ask the COIB to do so.

Feeling the pressure, my opposite number at the COIB, Laura Denman, joined the dance routine and announced that her agency would release the report if both DOI and Holtzman had no objection. Not one to deny myself the pleasure of the deftly completed side step, I announced, on Shepard's instructions, that DOI had no objection to such a release.

Our dance number completed, both DOI and the COIB bowed to Holtzman. It was her turn to click her heels and move on out of the way. Her response didn't say much for her composure, but it did say a great deal about the pressure she now felt herself under. While being interviewed on TV the next night, just five days before the election, she began crying and had to leave the set.

That same day, DOI completed the report. We had planned to have it ready early in the evening to send to the individual members of the Conflicts of Interest Board, but one or another fussy DOI attorney kept making last-minute changes in the sixty-three-page document. At about midnight, we were finally printing it when someone noticed that "September" was misspelled on the cover, and we had to start all over again.

Finally, we sent it in the middle of the night by separate couriers to the homes of all five members of the COIB. One COIB member lived so far out in the suburbs, and the courier became so lost, that the report was delivered to the fellow, an older man, as he sat in his kitchen waiting for it at 4 A.M. Unfazed by the hour, the old gentleman begin reading it as soon as it was handed to him. So did each of the other board members.

Losing sleep might not have helped the members of the board the next day, but one major player did regain her composure: Holtzman. She became her usual steely self and took a calculated gamble. She told interviewers she would not allow the release of the report before the election. Why not? Because it would be unfair to her and the voters to allow her opponents and the media to report on and interpret the report before the COIB had a chance to hold hearings on it. She also claimed the report was "unfinished" and "a working document," which it decidedly was not.

The real reason, of course, was that she needed only 40 percent of the vote to win the primary against Hevesi and Badillo and avoid any further tests at the polls until the general election. She calculated that she had almost enough support among black and liberal voters alone, to say nothing of women and Brooklynites, to keep her percentage that high. Trying to squeeze the last few percentage points out of a somewhat stony electorate, she apologized at the last moment, at a gathering of feminist leaders, for the vicious attack she had launched on Ferraro the year before. (Ironically, Holtzman had attacked Ferraro in part for not disclosing some of her own documents—her income tax returns.)

Holtzman's nervy gamble was a failure. Usually very few people vote in primary elections, and although more people came to the polls in this election than in many previous primaries, the extra people who came out were mostly those who felt angered and betrayed by Holtzman's apparent dishonesty. She had inadvertently given weight to their feelings by refusing to allow the release of the DOI report.

Alan "Who?" Hevesi won the primary, with Holtzman, the incumbent, coming in second, and Badillo trailing along in last place. Since Hevesi, although he came in first, hadn't won 40 percent of the vote, the rules called for a runoff to be held only two weeks later in which only Hevesi and Holtzman would compete.

With Badillo gone as a complicating factor and an even lower turnout predicted for the runoff, the momentum was clearly on Hevesi's side. But Holtzman continued to add to her trouble by underestimating DOI. The day after the primary, she authorized the release of the DOI report. After all, stonewalling had only hurt her. And DOI had always been a paper tiger; the report couldn't be that bad. If she could just get it out in the open and defuse any criticisms it might by chance contain of her, maybe she could tiptoe past Hevesi in the runoff.

It was a risky gamble, but Holtzman didn't know how risky. Written by a DOI much more independent than its predecessor, the report destroyed Holtzman's reputation. DOI had reviewed 15,000 documents and interviewed forty witnesses under oath. It said in its report that the evidence strongly suggested that Holtzman knew Fleet was attempting to get more bond business from the city when she asked it for the $450,000. At best, the report said, Holtzman had been "grossly negligent" if she had not known of her office's dealings with Fleet about the loan and at worse had lied about her own dealings with the bank.

The report pointed out that two months before Holtzman's campaign applied for the loan, she and her campaign director had met with three Fleet officials, who had lobbied for more bond business and handed over thousands of dollars in campaign contributions—in cash, in an envelope—to Holtzman staffers.

The report revealed that high-level staffers in Holtzman's office knew of Fleet's campaign to get more city business and that it was hard to believe Holtzman didn't know. Since the press release proclaiming that the bank had won the extra business had been issued by Holtzman's office as well as the mayor's, it was difficult to believe Holtzman hadn't known about the release. On top of all this, Holtzman herself had signed the official documents authorizing the award of the new business to the bank.

All Holtzman could think to do was claim ignorance and amnesia. She said she hadn't read the press release, that she hadn't read the documents she signed—even though Fleet's name was on the page to which she affixed her signature—that she had no memory of the meeting with the Fleet executives, and that she hadn't participated in selecting Fleet for the extra bond business.

After she got through denying everything, those who might have believed her for a few moments wondered what she did with her time, except attack Ferraro. Arranging for the sale of city bonds was a major function of the comptroller's office. Either she was guilty or she was inept.

At an hourlong press conference Holtzman called to defend herself, she was reduced to attempting to rebut reporters' questions, over and over again, with the same answers: "I don't remember," "I don't recall," "I have no memory of that," and "No one ever told me." Most original of all was her claim that "I didn't need to know" because, in her view, the interest rate on the loan was allegedly what any other person would have been charged. Therefore, she claimed, she was not obliged under the city charter to know anything about the loan. She ignored the fact that it was unlikely the bank would even have considered giving anyone else such a loan in such circumstances except the woman who could return the gift a thousand times over a few months later.

In denying all knowledge of her subordinates' actions and before that attempting to stonewall the release of a report revealing her complicity in a conspiracy, Holtzman had gone full circle. She had become Richard M. Nixon, the politician she had denounced almost a generation before.

In the few days she had left before the runoff, she tried to distract the voters by talking about her work on behalf of women and against Nazi war criminals. But her reputation had long rested on her claim of holier-than-thou integrity, and the report had shown how hollow that claim had become. DOI had exposed her as just another politician with her hand out.

Game to the end, Holtzman even tried a few last-minute swings at Hevesi. In one desperate move, she accused him of a conflict of interest because he was a professor at a campus of the City University of New York while at the same time serving as a state assemblyman. No one could figure out what she meant.

Just before the runoff, in a last-minute burst of political calculation, Holtzman commissioned a poll to see what might swing a few votes her way. The pollsters told her best bet was to apologize for taking the Fleet loan. She did, but the obvious insincerity of her apology—the poll she took before she apologized was reported along with her apology—negated her gesture.

Holtzman lost the runoff to Hevesi by a 2-1 margin and retired. She is now an attorney in private practice.

DÉJÀ VU ALL OVER AGAIN: DOI AND THE PVB

*There is no one so high or so low
as to be immune from investigation
by this committee.—Unnamed
lead character,* The Investigator

Donald Manes's suicide had established Susan Shepard's DOI.

The popular president of the Borough of Queens was found in January 1986 in a car near Shea Stadium, bleeding profusely after having stabbed himself in the wrist and the leg in a failed suicide attempt. He claimed he'd been kidnapped and cut up by the kidnappers, but two months later plunged a knife into his heart, finishing the job in his own kitchen.

What killed him was the Parking Violations Bureau scandal, which threatened Mayor Koch's political career as well. In a desperate and ultimately unsuccessful attempt to preserve his chances for reelection, Koch issued the executive order removing the inspectors general from the control of the commissioners whose departments they were supposed to be investigating and made them employees of DOI.

This made it possible for IGs working for an independent DOI to arrest the heads of the department they were investigating. It also made DOI a force to be reckoned with at the highest levels of government. But it didn't stop the very able perps in the PVB case from making a comeback try. And when they did, they came close to ruining the new DOI that had been erected on what we had thought were their graves. Their effort also caused a major public explosion, massive tension between DOI and city hall, and . . .

The original PVB scandal had revolved around the payment of thousands of dollars of bribes to Manes, Deputy Mayor Stanley Friedman, and PVB Deputy Director Geoffrey Lindenauer, among others, in return for the granting of PVB contracts to a firm known as Datacom Systems Corporation. The scandal led not only to Manes's suicide, but to the jailing of Friedman, former Transportation Commissioner Michael Lazar, and six others; the firing of three Datacom officials; and the replacement of the formerly popular Edward Koch with the city's first black mayor, David N. Dinkins.

Ironically, the second PVB scandal unseated Dinkins and put in office the prosecutor in the first PVB scandal, Rudy Giuliani. It was made by possible by publicity, which competes only with money as the motivating force behind every government action.

DOI under Koch had been tipped off to the original PVB scandal before it became public knowledge. But it failed to investigate it. An informed tipster conveyed what he knew of the scandal to a DOI investigator, who in the sloppy way of the old DOI, took notes on the margin of a memo describing another matter. Later, he discarded that memo, forgetting about the notes he had scribbled on it, and DOI's knowledge of the original scandal was taken out with the trash. The agency's role in the original PVB scandal was, therefore, both embarrassing and minor. (Smarting with the memory of this incident, Shepard's DOI would later complete the establishment of a computer system in which all DOI employees were required to enter any tips they received. The system was set up so the tip could be neither revised nor erased.)

That PVB II took place at all was only because Datacom, the evildoer firm at the center of PVB I, pulled off a major public relations trick that almost carried it through both scandals. Datacom was owned by Lockheed, the major military-industrial contractor. But Datacom's publicity people managed to keep that fact out of the papers and the fact that Lockheed owned the firm penetrated very few brains during PVB I. So when the men who ran the company wanted to try once again to get their snouts back into the trough of money that other people saw as city government, they renamed the company Lockheed Information Management Systems. The public remained blissfully unaware that this corporate nemesis of good government had returned to its old tricks.

Lockheed's Datacom during PVB I had paid bribes for parking-ticket-collection contracts. Lockheed's Datacom, or rather, Lockheed Information Management Systems during PVB II, attempted to corner the contract to process the tickets. The motivating factor in both scandals was the same: money. The city raked in more than $300 million a year from traffic tickets, its greatest source of revenue other than taxes, even though it managed to collect only half of all the fines due. Any organization that could insert its snout into that business from any direction could, if it were dishonest, rake off all the dishonest bucks it would ever need. Honest companies would not do much worse.

So using its new name and fielding a mostly new set of executives, the company began working toward its ultimate goal: landing the contract to process, for profit, the traffic tickets that the PVB, with its civil servants, was already processing for salaries alone. It waited for several years until it saw its chance. And then, once again, it began to proffer inducements. Wining and dining and job offering began.

The wait was necessary because DOI, in conjunction with several other city agencies, was required to check on every company that sought a city contract as soon as that company made its first formal move to do so. Since the city spends $2 billion a year on outside contracts, a lot of companies apply for a piece of the pie. But the city charter assigns the other agencies the bulk of the contractor-checking work. All DOI is required to do is check its files for the previous five years to see if it has completed an investigation of the applying company during those years. If no such investigation is found in its files, it reports just that. DOI performs 30,000 such file checks each year.

So when a relatively small city contract, a $10-million job of data processing for the PVB came up, Lockheed, seeing its chance to reestablish itself as a city contractor, applied for the contract and got it. There was no question that the company was qualified to bid and that it would do the job at a relatively reasonable price. It was its medium-term motives that were suspect. As soon as it had reestablished itself as a city contractor, its executives believed, it could compete for the extremely lucrative contract to process all the tickets.

The Dinkins administration was more than cooperative with Lockheed's attempt at rehabilitation. The mayor was anxious to show some signs of achievement as he reached the midterm mark. (The fact that he eventually achieved so little, other than freeing DOI for a spell and increasing the size of the Police Department, means that Dinkins's detractors were partly justified later on in referring to him as "just a social welfare hack.") Even a partial privatizing of the PVB would stand out in an otherwise lackluster mayoralty. High officials in the administration, knowing their jobs would rise or fall with Dinkins, began pushing hard for it.

Unfortunately, in their haste to get the job done and because of their many connections to the swarm of lobbyists, agents, and public relations people Lockheed had hired to work its way back into the city's good graces, they pushed Lockheed as the savior contractor and ignored other companies who, although just as qualified and interested, weren't as well connected. Among the administration officials operating this way was Philip Michael, the city budget director, an extremely powerful man in a city that spent $31 billion a year, much of it flowing through his fingers to the hungry heads of city agencies. Michael began his pressure campaign by leaning on the man in charge of the PVB, Transportation Commissioner Lucius Riccio, to give Lockheed the small contract as a way of paving the way for that company to get the big one.

Commissioner Riccio and Budget Director Michael didn't get along, and Riccio didn't appreciate the pressure Michael was putting on him. Riccio saw a chance not only for revenge but for getting Michael off his back when Michael, at a meeting at which numerous other city officials were present, loudly told Riccio that if he gave Lockheed the $10 million contract, Riccio's department would get a bigger budget. Riccio complained to *New York Newsday* that the budget director was pressuring him and appeared to be "running fast and loose" with city contracting procedures.

The newspaper published a story airing Riccio's complaints and Michael's rebuttal. In the story, reporter George E. Jordan also came close to dumping years of Lockheed PR labor down the drain by noting that Lockheed was the former Datacom of PVB scandal fame and that it was trying to work itself back into the city's good graces. No one noticed.

Well, not exactly no one. First Deputy Mayor Norman Steisel, who had supported Michael in his attempt to get the contract for Lockheed, turned purple, in private, and ordered Riccio to retract his charges, in writing. Showing himself to be the clever maneuverer he indeed was, Riccio wrote *Newsday* a letter in which he retracted what he had told its reporter without actually retracting his charges and slipped it passed the harried Steisel, who approved it.

Riccio also complained to DOI, which promptly investigated his allegations. A high-level DOI investigator interviewed Michael and everyone else present at the meeting. All of them except Riccio denied that any such comments had been made. Riccio insisted on his version, but the investigation was stymied.

Shepard, hoping for a break in the case, kept it open and kept sending investigators over to interview Riccio, asking if Michael or anyone else had put additional pressure on him to do any favors for Lockheed. He reported no more pressure, and eventually the case was closed. When further pressure *was* applied to him, he succumbed to it and told no one. Riccio could have resigned at this point, but after going through the experience of facing firing at Steisel's hands, he decided he'd rather keep his job than complain again. A quiet hush descended on the effort to enrich Lockheed at the expense of the taxpayers.

A few months later, however, Wayne Barrett wrote one of his incredibly long and detailed *Village Voice* articles—about Lockheed. The immense length and myriad of details usually made Barrett's articles difficult if rewarding reading.

Barrett sidestepped this problem in his article on Lockheed. He allowed a reporter for the *Daily News* to read it and summarize it in that newspaper the day before it appeared in the *Voice*, providing a vast public with a digest of the story it could understand and bringing Barrett's piece a larger audience than usual.

Barrett's article was based not on conjecture but on fact. Lockheed né Datacom was about to land a major PVB contract once again—the big one, not the little one that had inspired Riccio's initial complaint. It already, in fact, had been approved as the contractor, only the formalities had yet to be completed. And it seemed to have approached the landing of this contract the same way it had obtained its previous one—through influence-peddling, though this time more in the form of job offers, meals, and entertainment rather than bags of cash. Nevertheless, the resemblance between its performance in PVB I and in what was immediately recognized as PVB II was so strong, the public memory of PVB I so vivid, and the arrogance Lockheed was showing by going after the same honey pot once again, after months of unfavorable exposure in every form of media just a few years before, instantly made PVB II into a major scandal.

Suddenly, everybody was all over Dinkins. How could he let this happen under his own nose? Dinkins was shocked himself. A hands-off administrator, he probably hadn't known any of this was going on. He was appalled at the damage a PVB repeat could do to his chances for reelection, especially since it was occurring in, of all years, an election year. He immediately ordered any movement toward the contract suspended. He also ordered DOI to investigate.

DOI, a Dinkins administration agency, began the investigation that would lead only four months later to a massive report that condemned high Dinkins administration officials by name and helped to destroy the administration's reputation. High-level city officials were brought over to DOI headquarters and examined, under oath, by DOI attorneys. Documents written by DOI's superiors in the chain of mayoral command were subpoenaed and scrutinized. As DOI officials began to realize what the report would say, and what was likely to happen as a result of its release, they began to worry. "We're working ourselves out of business," one DOI official said. But the effort continued.

In the meantime, though, Riccio began to worry. Sure, he had initially brought the beginnings of PVB II to the public's attention, and to DOI's, but then he had decided to go along with the gang in order to keep his job. He had to find some way to protect himself before the ax descended heavily on his unprotected neck.

So, in an exclusive interview published in the *New York Times*, Riccio charged that hey, he had told DOI about the nascent PVB II scandal months before the *Voice* revealed it, but DOI had done nothing. His unspoken theme: DOI was to blame, not him, for the resurgence of the PVB nightmare. His charges drove Shepard into a frenzy. Suddenly, the reality of the free and honest DOI she had built and, perhaps more importantly, the image of a free and honest DOI, were threatened with destruction by a bureaucrat seeking to keep himself out of harm's way.

At a city council hearing on the PVB situation at which she was invited to testify, Shepard took the virtually unprecedented step of denouncing the *Times* for making a mistake—a major insult for a paper of that caliber—by not indicating the work DOI had done in attempting to verify Riccio's original complaints. She visited newspaper editorial boards all over the city, wrote letters, made statements, phoned everybody she could think of—and finally persuaded the *Times* to run a correction pointing out DOI's early role in the case.

In a sense, she needn't have bothered. As her investigators, including First Deputy Commissioner Alex Zigman, closed in for the kill, reporters sensed the fear at city hall and its undeniable corollary, the independence of DOI. The final DOI report, when released, established in the public mind the independent stature Shepard had achieved for the department.

The 209-page document revealed in great detail that Lockheed was being given preference on the PVB contract, that Budget Director Michael had showed favoritism toward Lockheed on numerous instances; that Lockheed, in an effort to snag the contract, had been luring Ellen Baer, Steisel's chief of staff with offers of future employment although she was a chief player in the contract negotiations; that Lockheed had failed to disclose that some of its current executives were involved, not so peripherally, in PVB I; that the company had lied on official forms in an effort to position itself for the contract . . . the list went on and on. A Lockheed executive, determined to show that the company would not be beaten, at least verbally, charged that every single allegation in the DOI report was wrong. But by then no one was listening to him.

Reaction to the report ranged from the sublime to the semiridiculous. The Kennedy School of Government at Harvard University requested and received DOI permission to include the report in its 1994 curriculum. Stanley Friedman, a major participant in PVB I, was so anxious to see the report that he said he was going to rush down to DOI headquarters to pick up a copy in person. He was finally persuaded that the risk of his being photographed picking up the PVB II report was too great. Did he really want to read a caption under his picture along the lines of "Stanley Friedman, sentenced to twelve years in jail in 1986 for his part in PVB I and since released, made haste to obtain a copy of the PVB II report so he could see how close others had come to repeating his feat"? And Jimmy Breslin, who compared the report to the book *Bonfire of the Vanities*, called from Jim Brady's bar across the street from DOI and asked that a copy of the report be delivered to him in person.

It was almost embarrassing how long the stories on the report continued to appear. After digesting the highlights of the document, but realizing that many more riches remained buried in it, some journalists started combing its fine print for more information on city corruption. This in itself was unusual since it was rare for more than a few extremely thorough reporters to read any part of any DOI report, much less plow through a 209-page tome and its numerous footnotes.

What was even more unusual and gratifying for them was that on second reading they found even more than they had discovered the first time through. One gem they noticed after the first frantic read-through was a footnote in which DOI mentioned that a top City Hall aide had said "I don't remember" thirty-seven times in a row when asked questions about relatively recent PVB events by DOI Special Counsel Andy Melnick, the lead investigator on the case and the principal author of the report, during a formal, under-oath interrogation at DOI headquarters.

The official, Donna Blank, arrogant, attractive, and intelligent, apparently realized after the report was issued that DOI meant business. Included in the footnote concerning her was a recommendation that she be disciplined for failure to cooperate with a DOI investigation by refusing to answer the questions. She asked and was granted permission to return to the agency and answer most of the questions she had claimed she couldn't remember the answers to a few weeks before.

Other gems were found in other footnotes. Like the original forty-niners (the prospectors, not the team), the reporters involved began to get overexcited. One kept calling me and screaming, "Do you stand by your footnote??? Do you stand by your footnote???" I think he'd seen *All the President's Men* once too often.

All of this folderol resulted in a sea of anti-PVB and antiadministration ink. Dinkins was left with no choice. He fired Michael, ordered hearings on the other violations DOI had pointed out, and put the kibosh on the Lockheed contract, which his administration had been on the verge of signing. Steisel demoted Baer and cut her salary by $10,000.

The old DOI had failed miserably to halt PVB I before it had siphoned millions of dollars from the treasury and corrupted major city officials. The new DOI had stopped the same company from getting its hands on any major city activity or any taxpayer money whatsoever.

Michael, Riccio, Steisel, Baer and all the other players in PVB II are now out of office, in large part because they touched the PVB incubus. And Giuliani, who prosecuted PVB I, rode PVB II into City Hall.

Not that everything will ever be A-OK in the world of city contracting. A story is told about the two crooked city contractors who have come to a bid-opening session at a city agency. Naturally, although illegally, they have informed each other of the amount they intend to bid on the various available jobs. Both have bid very high, but since their efforts were coordinated and they expect no other bidders, they hope to bag the jobs they want at a major and unnecessary cost to the taxpayers.

They and the city official who will collect their bids are sitting calmly in the bidding room waiting for the announced bid-opening time when a Japanese man unknown to any of them walks calmly into the room and sits down at the table with them. He takes a sheaf of envelopes from his briefcase. The two crooked contractors look at each other with fear in their eyes and slowly move their sealed bids off the table and back into their pockets. Just as slowly, they replace them with envelopes containing the much more realistic but much less profitable bids they had brought along in case other parties entered the bidding, an event they had worked for months to prevent.

The appointed time arrives, and the official announces the opening of bidding. He takes the new envelopes from the two now-pale contractors and looks expectantly at the Japanese man. That individual asks the city official if he is Kim Sykes. The official says he is not and gives him directions to Mr. Sykes's office on another floor. The Japanese man leaves, taking his envelopes with him, and the two contractors collapse.

AFTERMATH

You're on the road, the great American road!
—Voice-over from an auto company documentary
about the future of the automobile.

Out on Miller Road
—Common expression in Detroit meaning "fired" or
"laid off." Miller Road runs by a General Motors plant.

Former DOI commissioners haven't always traveled down the world's most apparently respectable roads. Kevin Frawley, one of Koch's better-looking DOI chiefs, became a Wall Street investor and then . . . a model. Cadillac was looking around for a face to put in its Lease-a-Caddy ads and chose Frawley's. The ad identified him as the first vice president of a major securities firm and quoted him as saying, "The best things in life aren't always free. Sometimes you have to lease them." If he had remained as DOI commissioner, "Sometimes you have to steal them" would have been more appropriate, in reference to the perps rather than to Frawley.

Another Koch-era DOI commissioner, Kenneth Conboy, left DOI to take a federal judgeship, later resigned his post to earn the money to put his kids through college, and surfaced recently investigating corruption in the District Council of New York City and Vicinity of the United Brotherhood of Carpenters and Joiners of America. (He seems to have discovered quite a bit. The head of the local was dismissed from his $360,000-a-year job by the national union president, who accused the ousted official of corruption and favoritism to mobsters.)

DOI also led its best commissioner down the road to unemployment. Susan Shepard, after letting Mayor Giuliani know she was not available for reappointment (as if he would have ever considered her), left DOI and joined her former second-in-command, Richard Daddario, in establishing a private investigations firm. It failed. She's now at home taking care of her kids. Andy Melnick, the principal author of DOI's PVB report, opened a similar firm in 1996 after sticking it out under the Giuliani administration for two years.

Daddario showed what he was made of when a would-be rabbi offered to put in a good word for him with Rudy's people so that he could retain his job at DOI under the new administration. Even though he had three young children to support, Daddario refused the offer of aid. He said accepting a job with Giuliani would make it appear as if DOI had completed and released the Holtzman, PVB, Ginger Man, and other reports only to curry favor with the incoming mayor. Shepard's selection would have conveyed the same impression, which is why she took the same action.

After the firm Daddario opened with Shepard went under, and after a year or so of unemployment, Daddario became an assistant United States attorney in New York and is now busily prosecuting drug cases.

John Kennedy, whose dog-walking habits led to my employment at the city's premier investigative agency, left during the Shepard administration to take a job as president of the Jewelry Security Alliance on Manhattan's Upper East Side. There, after years of helping the public secure its money against predators, he helps jewelers around the world protect their merchandise from thieves armed with glass cutters instead of fountain pens. He hired Bob Frank, who wrote both water-cop reports, to work under him.

Frank's boss, Bob Vinal, and Ellen Kay Schwartz, the cowboy-boot-wearing inspector general, both became administrative judges in the Police Department.

Much higher in Police Department headquarters was Ed Norris, the DOI detective who tried to uncover the Fire Department's alleged shenanigans at the World Trade Center. He was, appropriately enough, assigned to head the cold case squad (which attempts to solve cases other units have given up on) after he returned to the Police Department. He did so well at this and other jobs that by mid-1996, at age thirty-four, after being showered with promotions, he had became NYPD deputy commissioner for operations, one of the department's top honchos.

With Norris one of the few exceptions, those who were required by their job descriptions to fend off allegations of corruption did better than those who fought corruption.

Special Executive Assistant to the Mayor Ken Sunshine, who had been accused of trying to influence that department on behalf of the mayor's restaurant-owning buddies, opened his own public relations firm and took his place on the board of a nonprofit group that advocates on behalf of the poor.

Lee Jones, to some extent DOI's nemesis, became press secretary to Ruth Messinger, Manhattan's borough president and the leading Democratic mayoral candidate for 1997.

Joe DePlasco, who had the thankless job of fending off DOI's forays into the Parking Violations Bureau and other parts of the Transportation Department, also did well. He became press secretary to Public Advocate Mark Green, a possible mayoral candidate and probable U.S. senatorial candidate in the near future.

DOI AS LAP DOG

DOI is where government happens or not.
—Richard Murphy, former commissioner
of the Department of Youth Services,
investigated by both Shepard and Wilson.

And slowly answered Arthur
From the barge; the old order
Changeth, yielding place to new;
And God fulfills himself in many ways,
Lest one good custom should
Corrupt the world.
—Alfred, Lord Tennyson

Giuliani's plans for DOI had been best summarized before he took office, when someone asked him for his reaction to DOI's investigation of the Parking Violations Bureau while Dinkins was mayor. His response: "An administration out of control." What he meant was, it was an administration that couldn't even protect itself from its own investigators. In a nefarious way, he was right.

He replaced Shepard with Howard Wilson, an old and trusted friend and associate. Wilson started each and every day by faithfully attending the mayor's cabinet meetings, something Shepard, during the Dinkins years, had never done. Wilson could not possibly avoid being influenced by the mayor's nods and winks or by the nuances of the discussions among top Giuliani administration officials that took place at these daily gatherings.

In any case, Wilson's presence at these events was a symptom of a much more serious problem. As a DOI executive who served under both Shepard and Wilson said, "When the mayor asked Shepard to investigate something, her attitude would be, 'When we're finished with the investigation, we'll get back to you. If someone in your administration is involved, that's too bad . . .' This guy, it's all phone calls back and forth from city hall to DOI, who to talk to, who not to talk to . . . "

As a result of the calls, the cabinet meetings, and Wilson's ancient friendship with the mayor—a relationship totally dissimilar to that between any recent mayors and their DOI commissioners—DOI soon became closely synchronized with the goals and objectives of the rest of the administration, an impossible stance for an investigative body.

Although he can hardly be considered an unbiased source, David Dinkins, defeated by Giuliani in 1993, said in late 1996 that were he to have it to do all over again, he would once again appoint an independent Susan Shepard rather than a bosom buddy of his as DOI commissioner. "It's very important that the people have confidence in DOI and feel that no one is above the law," he said, "not the mayor or anyone else. DOI is supposed to investigate the mayor, the deputy mayor, or wherever the trail leads . . .

"You need loyal people in most positions, but for certain jobs, loyalty to the mayor should not be the criterion," the ex-Mayor said.

Under Giuliani, loyalty was not only a criterion, it was far and away the most important criterion of all. Although as relentless as usual at the lower levels of government, DOI soon reverted with a vengeance to what it had been at the higher levels of the city bureaucracy before Shepard took over—a friend of city hall, or, as one popular phrase had it, "*The Mayor's* Secret Police."

During Wilson's first few months I wondered how diligent controlled investigators would be. One day, shortly after I left DOI, I walked out of my new, private-sector office and a few blocks away saw a battered old truck from the Parks and Recreation Department parked in the street. The two men in the cab were wearing work clothes and appeared to be shooting the breeze while they ate lunch from paper bags. Nothing would have struck me as unusual about the scene except that I recognized them as DOI investigators.

I ambled over to talk to them and listened stone faced as they tried to make me believe they had taken new jobs at half their former pay with Parks and Recreation as a result of the latest municipal fiscal crisis, although it was obvious they were watching who went in and out of a nearby government office. I started laughing and after a while so did they, although they never admitted anything.

I was glad to see the agency was still on the watch, but I still felt uneasy. As long as Giuliani was mayor, I thought, no agents would ever stake out City Hall, metaphorically or otherwise.

Wilson, in fact, did the exact opposite, and not at all metaphorically. He staked out, harassed, and tormented Giuliani's enemies. When Act Up, an AIDS group, objected to a decision by Deputy Mayor Fran Reiter to institute savage cuts in public assistance for

AIDS patients, DOI decided to investigate Housing Works, an Act Up subsidiary that happened to be within DOI's purview because it received some city funds.

The resulting presence of DOI investigators at the subsidiary's Manhattan offices for three weeks, and the publicity resulting from the investigation, "sent every single funder into a panic," according to Charles King, the subsidiary's chief executive. Housing Works, which concentrates on helping AIDS patients, had not recovered financially by 1997. And DOI, in line with what soon became its standard practice in its political investigations, issued no report on the investigation nor arrested anyone as a result of it. What would seem to be the investigation's real goal—harassing the mayor's opponents (or, in other cases, embalming his critics with the promise of an investigation)— had been fulfilled.

"If you don't want to get investigated, don't criticize the government," said a New York Civil Liberties Union official, when asked about the Housing Works investigation. These words should have become DOI's new motto.

Giuliani's DOI didn't just want to befuddle and confuse his opponents. It wanted to hide the administration's own sins. For all the mayor's attempts to appear as Cleanest of the Clean, his administration, even more so than its predecessors, soon showed itself to be hellbent on rewarding its supporters in the community not only with high-paying jobs but with millions of dollars in taxpayers' money. Surprisingly for a business-oriented mayor, Giuliani seemed intent not only on rewarding his friends in the business world but also on rewarding those social service groups that could be counted on to support him in his reelection campaign and other political struggles. (Using social services groups for this purpose is much easier than in years past. The government-supported social-services sector has grown huge in recent decades, and the parameters for the services such agencies provide—such as finding jobs for the unemployed and counseling welfare recipients—are so flexible as to make politicizing their selection an easy task.)

Selecting barely adequate social service groups as recipients of juicy contracts because of their support for the mayor, along with the direct and more traditional hiring of political darlings for high-paying city jobs in order to preserve their skills and loyalty for reelection service, may be so prevalent in the Giuliani administration as to constitute its Achilles heel. And DOI has been delegated to run behind the administration and attack anyone who approaches this weak spot.

This became apparent, when, as part of an attempt to divert the press' attention from the resignation of Rev. John Brandon, Giuliani's Youth Services commissioner, who had been charged with not paying his taxes, Giuliani ordered DOI to investigate not Brandon but Richard Murphy, who had been Dinkins's Youth Services commissioner. The mayor's aides accused Murphy of having overspent his agency's budget and of having arranged a break-in at his own offices to destroy the evidence of his overspending.

Giuliani's motive, of course, was to mask the administration's desire that millions of dollars in Youth Services contracts be transferred to groups that supported him. This politically motivated transfer, which soon took place under cover of the attack on Murphy, caused a number of legitimate youth services groups to close their doors and fire their staffers as their city checks were suddenly cut off and the money shifted to other groups.

Although DOI exonerated Murphy long after the administration's goal—the transition to pro-Giuliani social services groups—had been achieved, it pointedly avoided questioning Deputy Mayor Ninfa Segarra, who had administered the transition from one set of youth groups to the other.

"The whole Youth Services thing was political," former Mayor Koch said. Koch is also biased, but his words in this case are worth hearing. "What they accused Youth Services of [the overspending and the cover-up burglary] had not happened."

The administration's aim of ensuring, with DOI's help, maximum support for the mayor's reelection campaign became even more apparent when DOI found itself forced to investigate allegations appearing in *New York Newsday* that William Koeppel, a tony Manhattan landlord, had given rent breaks and discounts to Giuliani campaign staffers when Giuliani was running for office in 1993. Koeppel was also accused of giving various breaks to tenants who agreed to contribute to the Giuliani election effort.

One of those tenants had complained about this practice during the campaign. Wilson, at the time an adviser to the campaign, had ordered her contribution returned. Then, after Wilson had become DOI commissioner, his agency was forced to investigate the propriety of Koeppel's conduct when it was asked to do so by the Conflicts of Interest Board.

The agency then began investigating a practice that its boss, Wilson, obviously had known about while the practice was underway. This was a return to the practice in many city agencies before Koch laid the groundwork for DOI's short-lived independence. Lap-dog investigators were investigating their own bosses.

Wilson recused himself from the investigation, but his recusal had little effect on the staff dependent on him for raises, promotions, and tenure that then took over the probe. In any case, by the time DOI began investigating the scandal, no one at the highest or lowest levels of DOI, or anyone in the city with the slightest bit of interest in the subject, could even pretend to be ignorant of the mayor's strongly held and publicly announced view on what the outcome of the investigation should be—that all those who received the rent breaks were innocent. No one was surprised when DOI came to that conclusion.

One of Koeppel's rewards for his loyalty, perseverance, and fund-raising efforts came when Giuliani appointed him to the board of directors of the city's Off-Track Betting Corporation. Soon thereafter, when an OTB employee went to DOI with allegations of scandal at the race track agency, he complained in a lawsuit that DOI had let OTB know he had gone to the formerly closed-mouth investigative agency with the information.

DOI's motivating fear that the administration's continuing effort to shift tax money to politically friendly social services groups would be halted also monopolized DOI's attention in a scandal involving a former employee of the city's Community Development Agency. DOI subpoenaed her, not to ask her about the contract-shifting process, but to grill her about how some journalists had learned that the administration was planning to shift various service contracts administered by the CDA to groups supporting the mayor.

Social services contracts were also behind what became the FBI's public affirmation of DOI's new subservient status. After political influence in the awarding of $43 million in social services contracts to the Hellenic-American Neighborhood Action Committee, a pro-Giuliani group, had been publicly revealed, DOI was forced to begin probing the mess. But the FBI, seeing the seriousness of the scandal, concluded that DOI could not investigate it independently, such a creature of city hall had DOI become. The federal agency then took the locally unprecedented step of forcing DOI to step aside and taking over the investigation itself. In doing so, the FBI noted that Wilson had repeatedly briefed the mayor on the investigation's progress during DOI's short-lived administration of the probe.

The enthusiastic, hard-working Wilson, however, couldn't seem to stop himself from working in the mayor's reelection campaign even after the FBI had put him on notice. Although Wilson insisted it was inadvertent, DOI forwarded information about the employees of Guiliani's potential 1997 mayoral rivals, gained through its charter-mandated background checks, to top city hall officials.

Meanwhile, DOI resources that weren't being used to ensure the mayor's reelection were squandered on . . . supervision of construction. In the words of a mayor's office press release, Wilson, as commissioner of investigation "oversaw vital management initiatives to improve the construction of streets, roads and bridges. Additionally, he worked with Con Edison in substantially reducing the time spent, per location, on the replacement of steam pipes. He also reviewed and analyzed the process for new traffic signals throughout the city, reducing installation and approval time. . . . " As former Mayor Koch said when told of this, "Construction management!!?? DOI doesn't have any expertise in that area at all."

Considering its agenda, it wasn't surprising that DOI didn't want the public to know what it was doing. The *Daily News*, usually a supporter of the administration, was so frustrated by this policy that it sued DOI for refusing to release information the agency routinely had revealed under several pre-Giuliani administrations. The affair began when *News* reporter David Lewis filed a Freedom of Information request for all the closing memos DOI had issued during 1994. Closing memos, the reports completed by DOI investigators at the end of each investigation, had been routinely released under previous administrations.

Although under the previous mayors such documents had been edited — "redacted," in legal jargon—to protect the names of sources, witnesses, and those against whom evidence had not been found, they *were* released and always resulted in unflattering stories about city corruption.

It looked at first as if Wilson's DOI would, in this one instance, follow in the footsteps of its predecessors. DOI officials first told Lewis the agency was working on his request. Then they denied him all the reports. A strained meeting between *News* and city hall bigwigs ensued, as a result of which Lewis was allowed to have the paper the memos were printed on. The redactors at DOI had

gone wild with their black felt-tip pens. What they accomplished
with their redactions was to make most of the memos worthless.
They refused even to release redacted versions of seventy-seven
of the hundreds of memos involved.

Daily News Managing Editor Arthur Browne said that DOI's
action, which his newspaper had gone to court to overturn, would
cause, if allowed to remain in place, "a long-term detrimental
effect on the public's right to know what is happening in New
York City government."

In keeping with the mayor's intention to hold his DOI ace
close to his vest, DOI's reports, even those on scandals predat-
ing Giuliani's inauguration, were dropped into a bottomless pit
from which they did not emerge. Soon after the new mayor took
over, he announced that although millions had been spent on a
new Kings County Hospital, only a hole in the ground had
appeared to show for the city's efforts. He ordered DOI to investigate. But you have to wonder what he said in private. His first
four-year term in office is now almost over, and the Kings County
Hospital report has not yet been released.

He ordered another report on alleged tampering with water
purity tests at the Environmental Protection Department after the
allegations were revealed by the *Daily News*. The investigation was
completed, and the report was written, but remained in the dark-
est of DOI's vaults in 1997. Also unreleased was a report on the
Fire Department's expenditure of millions of dollars on the purchase of two fireboats that couldn't fight fires. So was a report
on the death of a woman for whom an ambulance had been called
but who waited an hour and a half for it to arrive. The list goes
on and on.

Some may argue that Giuliani's later appointment of Fire
Commissioner Howard Safir as police commissioner might have
prompted the mayor not to release the fireboat report out of reluctance to embarrass a person he was moving from one major

appointment to another. But there are no such explanations to accompany the numerous other reports "in the hole." It's possible that Giuliani, in spite of all his law-enforcement cant, doesn't want DOI to do anything about higher-level law enforcement at all, in the same way President Reagan, despite his oratory to the contrary, didn't want the Environmental Protection Agency to protect the environment or many other federal government agencies to function in any way whatsoever. More likely, however, in an administration as obsessed as his with control, the mayor received summaries of the reports from Wilson and never revealed the commissioner's findings to the public—or to prosecutors.

Meanwhile, paradoxically, Gov. George Pataki, a more conservative Republican than Giuliani, thrived on exposes of his predecessor's antics and seemed so pleased with investigations in general that he redrafted former Mayor Koch's Executive Order 105, signed it with his own name, and reorganized the state inspector general's office under its provisions.

Under this order, the state's twenty-nine inspectors general were told to report solely to the state's chief inspector general. They previously had been reporting to the heads of the departments they investigated as well as to the top IG. The governor dryly noted that "this change will strengthen their effectiveness."

Also, taking a leaf from DOI's book, the directive expanded the state inspector general's mandate to include the investigation of all allegations of criminal activity and conflicts of interest by state employees, as well as the corruption, fraud, and abuse the inspector general had previously been required to investigate. The order also required all state employees to report wrongdoing promptly to the state inspector general and promised "whistleblower" protection to all who did so.

In conjunction with promulgating this order, Pataki appointed a woman to the state's top investigative post for the first time in state history. If actually given her freedom, the new state inspector general, Roslynn Mauskopf, is likely to find a lot going on in Albany to occupy her and her newly energized investigators. Nothing of the kind is likely to be occurring in Giuliani's Gotham.

Giuliani finally realized, however, that the fuss his opponents would make over his use of DOI as a political club would itself hurt his reelection chances. A school-overcrowding crisis in the fall of 1996 gave him a chance to move Wilson away from DOI without seeming to humiliate his old friend. Wilson was returned to full-time private practice with his old law firm and part-time unsalaried work as the chairman of the city's School Construction Authority.

In his place, the mayor appointed Edward Kurianksy, whom he had known for twenty years but who was not as close a friend as Wilson had been. Kuriansky had served from 1981 to 1995 as the state's deputy attorney general and special prosecutor for Medicaid Fraud Control until he was dismissed by Dennis Vacco, Governor Pataki's attorney general, to make way, ironically enough, for patronage appointees.

Kuriansky seemed qualified. He had directed an eighteen-month undercover investigation that resulted in the indictment and conviction of more than fifty nursing home officials and their suppliers for involvement in extensive kickback schemes. But in another way he seemed more in the Giuliani-Wilson mold. The big breakthrough in nursing home prosecutions had been the work of Charles Hynes, who became Brooklyn district attorney, and Andrew Stein, who became speaker of the city council. They had convicted a real baddy—Bernard Bergman, a notorious nursing home operator—opening the door for future prosecutions.

Kuriansky was, at best, their clean-up man. The Medicare fraud office under his administration went after all the obvious cases that Hynes and Stein had made it possible to prosecute. But it never pursued the really difficult, really big cases in the field.

In fact, in an era of escalating fraud, the office under Kuriansky was described as "sleepy."

A sleepy DOI, at least when it came to investigating the Giuliani administration's social-services-group strategy, would be perfect for Mayor Giuliani. It would be far less than perfect for the taxpayers, and for the still sizable number of honest people in government. Maybe Kuriansky will shake off the doldrums and show real independence in his new assignment. If he does, he may be able to return DOI to its glory days. If he does not, DOI will remain in the dumpster, much too humble a place for an agency that rose so high.

ECHOES FROM ELSEWHERE

Although DOIs exist only in New York and Chicago, scandal exists everywhere in America. Some of the scandals resemble those revealed by DOI. Such scandals seem to turn up less frequently outside New York and Chicago, but that's probably because there aren't DOIs in other cities to uncover them. Some have surfaced, however. For instance:

Those people astute enough not be surprised that Chicago has preceded New York in at least some forms of corruption will not be shocked to learn that employees of the Chicago treasurer's office, including that office's head cashier, played a variant on the Sidberry caper described in Chapter 6 ("Bicoastal

Bonanza") four years before Sidberry began his drives through Los Angeles.

The Chicago perps used a simpler version of the Sidberry formula. They wrote official checks to each other on treasurer's office accounts that had since been closed and cashed them at the treasurer's office. When the bank bounced a check, they or their coconspirators would merely intercept and destroy the returned check before it reached an honest treasurer's office official.

A less-imaginative person might have looked upon this scheme as easily detectable and doomed from the start. But such a person would not have been familiar with the Chicago treasurer's office, which until recently had six incompatible computer systems totaling its accounts, making it impossible to take a balance of the office's fund. When Treasurer Miriam Santos combined the systems and took the office's first balance, she noticed the discrepancy and called in Chicago Inspector General Alexander Vroustouris.

Vroustouris, Shepard's nearest equivalent in the United States, arrested seven Chicago city employees after due investigation and charged them with stealing almost $50,000 through the scheme. Some of them had been on the job for twenty or thirty years and may have stolen much more than $50,000 over the course of their careers. In any case, the scheme had been successful enough that word of it had trickled down to the next generation. One of the perps, the daughter of another, was only twenty-eight years old and cashed her first bad check eight days after being hired by the city. Perhaps a long career in crime was snuffed out in the bud by Vroustouris's arrests.

Indicted by the state's attorney on charges of theft, deceptive practice, conspiracy, and forgery, six of the seven criminals pleaded guilty and were sentenced to terms ranging from one year to thirty months on probation. These terms would have been mild slaps on the wrist except that the perps also were required to return what they stole—the worst part of most white-collar sentences—in amounts ranging from $4,100 to $15,700 each. Three of them apparently were unable to keep up their restitution payments, or violated their probation in other ways, and were, in two cases, resentenced to longer terms of probation with 500 hours of community service thrown in. The only real loser was the one perp in the case who demanded a jury trial. After the man was found guilty by the jury, the judge took judicial note of his long criminal record and sentenced him to five years in the slammer.

———

Americans are so addicted to automobiles and motorists are so desperate for places to park, whatever the consequences, that every corner of the parking and traffic ticket business is full of juicy little plums ripe for the picking by businesspeople who some might say resemble some of those involved in New York City's PVB scandal.

Judging by an investigation done by the Houston city controller, George Greanias, some of the less-than-perfect businesspeople involved in the parking ticket business there were also involved in ripping off the city through its affirmative action program.

A firm called Municipal Collections was hired by Houston in 1993 to collect delinquent parking and traffic fines for the city. In Houston, as elsewhere, this is a big business. MC's officials knew they would be required to make about 22,000 phone calls a month to traffic and parking scofflaws and to mail off about 25,000 delinquency notices a month.

The city's affirmative action program required participation in contracts of this size by minority enterprises. MC arranged for a company owned by a Latina woman to subcontract some of the business from them—the printing and mailing of notices to scofflaws. But on presenting their bid to the city, they were told that a company called Bayou City Enterprises would be the only acceptable subcontractor. City officials insisted, in fact, that Bayou City be mentioned by name as the subcontractor in the contract between MC and the city and that it be guaranteed 19 percent of contract revenues, both unusual steps.

A couple of years after the contract was signed, Greanias attempted a routine audit of the Bayou City firm, a standard part of his job. When he asked the Bayou executives for the usual pile of paperwork to audit—utility expense records, rent records, management reports, quarterly payroll tax returns—all they were able to provide him were bills they had received from a third company, Premier Industries, which had actually printed and mailed the letters involved, and deposit slips indicating they had deposited checks they had received from MC.

Greanias decided that the Bayou Firm had done no work except take its cut of the hundreds of thousands of dollars for the job actually being done by MC and Premier. The controller refused to pay Bayou any more of the taxpayers' money.

A political squabble ensued as local minority businesses claimed that Bayou City was being held to higher standards than white businesses would have been. However, Greanias kept pointing out that Bayou City was being given public money for doing nothing, which was against the law.

Everyone denied that the president of Bayou City being the uncle of a prominent city council member had anything to do with this provision in the contract. Mayor Bob Lanier said that Bayou City was written into the contract at the insistence of several city council members, but the mayor's office employees involved insisted they couldn't remember the names of those members.

Mayor Lanier, trapped between angry taxpayers and angry affirmative action advocates, decided he could satisfy both sides by criticizing Greanias for assuming that the firm was doing nothing just because it couldn't prove it was doing something. Hav-

ing said this, he went ahead and canceled the Bayou City contract anyway, on the grounds that Greanias's refusal to give the
money to Bayou would delay the city's attempt to collect its overdue money from scofflaws.

A NOTE
OF CAUTION

I am looking for an honest man.
—Diogenes

Some time ago, long before I joined DOI, I started talking to the fellow in the seat next to me on an airplane. He was drinking fairly heavily. I was a newspaper reporter at the time, but I didn't tell him that. He was a purchasing agent for a large company. Several purchasing agents at other large private companies had recently been indicted for various offenses in various purchasing scandals. I asked him if any of what I had been reading about their activities was true.

He exploded. "Is any of it true!? It's all true! How do you think we get people to buy anything from us rather than the next guy? It's all bribes, trips, parties, women, liquor, drugs, whatever. I tell ya, it drives me nuts." He went on, but you don't want to know the details. So much for the morals of private industry, I thought.

187

Other personal and official data bear this out. In the relatively brief time I had access to corporate doings at a publishing company that put out one of my previous books and at one of the newspapers I worked for, several employees were fired for embezzlement. On one of the two occasions in my life I've filed an auto insurance claim, the adjuster offered me an inflated settlement if I agreed to kick back half the settlement to him.

Twice when I've hired people to steam-clean my couch, they've tried to triple their original estimate once they arrived at my apartment, each insisting in exactly the same words that "the girl at the office is new so she didn't know what she was doing when she took your order." All these people were private, not government employees. Many Americans, to say nothing of foreigners, could produce similar anecdotal histories as long as your arm.

Even though private employees may be as corrupt, or more so, than public employees, and the private sector is many times the size of the public sector, private corruption is rarely revealed, and if it is, it rarely causes outrage. It's rarely revealed because reporters find it very difficult to pierce the corporate veil and shine their pocket flashlights on the corruption beyond.

They find it much easier to reveal the waste of, as well as corrupt acts performed with, taxpayers' money. And, of course, readers are more interested in such stories since they see it as their money involved, not that of some anonymous corporate stockholder. (Although you could easily argue that everyone who has ever purchased anything has contributed to private corruption because the costs of such corruption are included in the prices we pay for everything, as well as in tax deductions granted corporations and in public funds paid them.)

Because DOI's job is to investigate and arrest people who steal money from or commit crimes against the city government, virtually all of what you've read deals with corruption involving taxpayers' money and public employees.

But now that you've read it, you should probably begin muttering to yourself, "There's probably a lot more private corruption out there than public corruption, but I'll never know very much about it, even though I myself will be its unknowing victim."

Maybe doing so will put what you've read in perspective.

DOI EXECUTIVE, INVESTIGATIVE, AND MANAGEMENT STAFF, DECEMBER 1993*

Susan E. Shepard, Commissioner
Richard C. Daddario, First Deputy Commissioner
Andrew B. Melnick, General Counsel

INVESTIGATIONS BUREAU:

Robert T. Brackman, Deputy Commissioner
Alex J. Zigman, First Assistant Commissioner
Michael L. Caruso, Assistant Commissioner/Correctional Services
Martha R. Hochberger, Assistant Commissioner/Inspection,
    Licenses & Permits
Steven A. Pasichow, Assistant Commissioner/Public Assistance
    & Grants
Vincent E. Green, Supervising Inspector General/Procurement,
    Real Property, Parks & Finance

---

*From New York City Department of Investigation, "Report to the Mayor, 1990-1993."

Lt. Edward T. Norris, Commanding Officer/Squad

Dennis T. Curran, Inspector General/Department of Buildings

Janice English, Inspector General/Housing Authority

Brian D. Foley, Inspector General/Consumer Affairs and Taxi & Limousine Commission

Joseph E. Gubbay, Inspector General/Economic Development and Special Assignments

Peggy Anne Heinkele, Director/Marshal's Bureau

Thomas McCormack, Inspector General/Department of Housing Preservation & Development

Keith Schwam, Inspector General/Department of Sanitation

Ellen Kay Schwartz, Inspector General/Department of Transportation

Kyle R. Sturcken, Inspector General/Department of Health

Robert W. Vinal, Inspector General/Department of Environmental Protection

Susan L. Ross, Deputy Assistant Commissioner

David W. Burke, Director/Corruption Prevention and Management Review

Marvin Putterman, Director/Investigative Audit

MANAGEMENT AND BUDGET:

Terry K. McClain, Deputy Commissioner

Dyrnest K. Sinckler, Assistant Commissioner/Administration

BACKGROUND INVESTIGATIONS & RECORDS MANAGEMENT

Philip D. Osattin, Assistant Commissioner

OTHER BIG DOI CASES*

FRAUDULENT SURETY BONDS ("DOUBLE INDEMNITY")

DOI conducted investigations, resulting in the arrest and conviction of six persons, involving the submission of fraudulent performance and payment bonds by construction and maintenance contractors doing business with city agencies. These bonds are required by state law and protect the city against losses caused by contractors who are unable to complete work.

Fraudulent bonds have been found in more than 70 contracts let over a five-year period, with aggregate contract values of $85 million and aggregate premium values of approximately $1.5 million. The city recovered $963,352 from contractors and stopped payments of $1.1 million to contractors who did not have legitimate bonds.

In response to DOI's recommendation, the Department of General Services now confirms the authenticity of bonds directly with

---

*From New York City Department of Investigation, "Report to the Mayor, 1990-1993."

the surety company rather than the broker, and consults the directory published by the State Insurance department to ensure that the bonds are issued by companies licensed to do business in New York. DOI also requested that the Mayor's Office of Risk Management issue a memo to all city agencies regarding the few straightforward steps that should be taken to verify the authenticity of bonds.

HPD MAINTENANCE CONTRACTS ("IN-REM")

In April 1991, and January 1992, DOI arrested 14 persons, including eight employees of the Department of Housing Preservation and Development and six private contractors on bribery charges in connection with the award of contracts for maintenance and repair work at city-owned buildings. HPD, which manages more than 4000 residential buildings owned by the city as a result of tax foreclosures, awards contracts for jobs like replacing doors or window panes, painting hallways and deleading walls and ceilings. The HPD employees arrested, who were responsible for awarding contracts under $10,000, received bribes in exchange for awarding nearly $200,000 worth of contracts.

14TH STREET RECONSTRUCTION PROJECT ("14TH STREET")

In November 1993, a report, prepared by DOI's Corruption Prevention and Management Review Bureau, revealed that an engineering firm hired by the Department of Transportation to supervise the $23 million reconstruction of 14th Street, from Avenue C to the Hudson, in Manhattan, performed incompetently and that DOT failed to adequately monitor and supervise the engineering firm's work.

It was revealed that nearly 25 percent of 800 loads of concrete poured to reconstruct the roadbed between July 3 and September 13, 1991 was substandard. While tests conducted by the engineering firm which was paid $1.6 million to serve as DOT's representative at the site, revealed that the concrete was substandard, the firm did not stop the continued pouring, or demand that it be removed, or report its use to DOT. In addition, the resident engineer assigned to the project falsely certified that all materials supplied and work performed were fully in compliance with the provisions.

DOT managers were criticized for assigning a relatively inexperienced staff engineer to manage this and eight other projects. DOT also failed to hold the engineering firm accountable for its failures before assigning its own staff to supervise the project.

The report also found that numerous safety hazards were created by the reconstruction in 1990 and 1991, including unbarricaded materials, blocked access to fire hydrants, non-working street lights and signals, unremoved debris and unfilled potholes and excavations.

The report contained eleven recommendations to DOT to correct the management weaknesses identified.

WATER METERING PROGRAM ("VANGUARD")

In November 1991, Vanguard Meter Services and four company executives were indicted on charges stemming from their scheme to defraud the city's $290-million water meter installation program. The investigation, which was conducted with the Manhattan District Attorney's Office and the federal Office of Labor Racketeering, revealed that Vanguard paid installers on a piecework basis rather than prevailing wage rates as required by city contract provisions. Vanguard also falsely represented that it performed pre-plumbing work under the supervision of licensed plumbers.

The investigation stopped a continuing fraud of approximately $1 million per year. In addition at the time of Vanguard's indictment, Vanguard was still owed $6 million by the Department of Environmental Protection. The money has been retained by the city until all potential claims have been settled and the city determines the total damages of the fraud, which could be as great as the total value of the contracts obtained.

DOI recommended changes in the manner in which contracts under DEPs Universal Metering Program are monitored to insure contractor compliance. As a result, DEP instituted new contract controls and review procedures. DEP now requires all meter installation contractors to provide certified payrolls verifying compliance with the prevailing wage law.

Purchase of Goods and Services

The city spends approximately $2 billion per year for supplies, materials, equipment, rent, utilities, contractual and consultant services, and other purchases of goods and services. Although the Department of General Services is the city's primary procurement agency, every city agency is involved in purchasing. Corruption, fraud or theft can occur in any city agency at any stage of the procurement process, from the initial preparation of specifications to the entry of goods into city inventory. DOI's Procurement Unit, which encompasses the Inspector-General's Office for DGS, is the department's central repository of expertise on the city's procurement policies, rules and procedures.

HRA CONTRACTS FOR CAR SERVICES ("BIG APPLE")

In 1990, DOI made 40 arrests in an investigation of wholesale billing fraud by Big Apple car service, which, under a contract with HRA since 1984, transported abused and neglected children to HRA facilities throughout the City. The fraud involved the submission of invoices for trips never taken [including some trips allegedly taken by "Greta Garbo"] and was encouraged by HRA's failure to audit the contract and to follow standard procedures for verifying billings.

The cost of the Big Apple contract, the larger of two HRA contracts for car services, escalated steadily during the period 1985-1988, reaching a high of $6 million in FY '88. As a result of DOI's investigation, fraud control measures were implemented and car service costs substantially reduced. The total cost of these car services decreased from approximately $9 million in 1988 to $4.5 million. In addition, the court-ordered restitution against fifteen defendants in the amount of $130,000 and an additional $40,000 in judgments against five defendants is outstanding.

DEPARTMENT OF CORRECTION CONTRACTS ("JENKINS")

In October 1992, William Jenkins, an assistant commissioner with the Department of Correction was arrested on charges that he took $24,000 in kickbacks from a Long Island cleaning supply company in exchange for awarding it 24 contracts worth $238,000. The DOC official, who also received quantities of toilet paper [apparently for his own use], only accepted bids from the company or one of several "fronts" established to make it appear that there was competition for the contracts.

Jenkins, who was terminated from his position with DOC, was charged with extortion under the federal Hobbs Act, and sentenced to one year in prison.

In addition, in August 1993, a correction officer assigned to Jenkins' unit was charged with accepting payments from another janitorial supply company in Queens to certify that it delivered supplies to DOC when in fact it had not.

PROCUREMENT FOR ELECTRONIC MONITORING SERVICES ("BL")

In May 1992, DOI issued a report criticizing two Department of Correction officials for their roles in DOC's efforts to procure electronic monitoring services, which allow DOC to monitor defendants participating in a "house arrest" program as an alternative to incarceration. The report revealed that violations of city purchasing regulations were so severe that DOC's chief contracting officer may have been improperly influenced to manage the negotiations in a way that benefited a Colorado vendor in its selection as the low bidder on the $1.9 million contract.

The contracting officer's errors undermined the competitiveness and fairness of the procurement process. The report also criticized a DOC Assistant Commissioner for attending staff meetings involving the award of the contract even though the Colorado vendor was represented by her former employer.

The report recommended clarification of certain provisions of the Procurement Policy Board rules, particularly rules governing amendments and best and final offers once the evaluation process has begun. The contract was rebid and, in August 1992, awarded to another company at a cost significantly lower than the initial contract.

MISMANAGEMENT AT GRACIE MANSION ("HEADBOARD")

In February 1991, DOI's Corruption Prevention and Management Review Bureau completed a review, requested by the Mayor, of expenditures at Gracie Mansion. The review followed news reports concerning the construction of a headboard for the Mayor's bedroom by city workers. DOI found that $8.3 million in purchases involving four city agencies and costs for labor by a cadre of workers from seven city agencies had been spent at the mansion in the eight years prior to the review. One of the workers was a carpenter employed by the Human Resources Administration who expended approximately $11,000 in labor and materials to make a headboard. The report concluded that work was routinely ordered by Mayoral aides, often (as in the case of the headboard) without the Mayor's knowledge, and performed without proper oversight or control. As a result of the review, purchases and work assignments were more closely controlled and reviewed to help ensure that city workers are not being diverted from more essential tasks, such as construction of homeless shelters and maintenance of parks.

DEP PHONY PURCHASE ORDERS ("INVISIBLE INK")

Following allegations of procurement fraud at the Department of Environmental Protection, DOI set up an undercover office supply company, with the assistance of the FBI, which resulted in the July 1993 arrests of two DEP employees on federal conspiracy and embezzlement charges. The employees, whose combined city employment totaled 25 years, encouraged the undercover company to submit 12 invoices to DEP for office supplies. Only four orders were actually delivered. In return for approving the remaining eight purchase orders, totaling $15,000, the employees demanded kickbacks in the form of cash ($8,000) a television, VCR and wall unit.

INSPECTIONS AND CODE ENFORCEMENT

The city employs approximately 3700 inspectors, 800 supervisors, 175 managers and 1000 support personnel in agencies that conduct inspections and issue permits and licenses in connection with the enforcement of city codes and regulations. These agencies include the Departments of Buildings, Fire, Health, Consumer Affairs, Sanitation, Environmental Protection, Transportation, Housing Preservation and Development, Taxi and Limousine Commission, and Business Services.

Bribery and extortion are crimes that have long plagued city agencies that conduct inspections. DOI's success in combating inspectional corruption has continued since 1990 with investigations of organized corruption at the Department of Buildings, the Taxi and Limousine Commission and the Department of Sanitation.

EXTORTION BY BUILDINGS INSPECTORS ("JERICO")

Following a joint investigation by DOI and the Federal Bureau of Investigation, 30 inspectors and supervisors in DOB's Construction Unit were arrested on federal charges of conspiring to extort in excess of $150,000 over a three-year period from building owners, contractors and other licensed professionals to expedite inspections performed prior to the issuance of certificates of occupancy ("C of Os"). The Department of Buildings administers and enforces building and zoning laws in the construction and alteration of buildings in the city. No building may be used or occupied unless a C of O has been issued.

The inspectors were charged with violating the federal Hobbs Act which bars public officials from extorting money in exchange for performing their official duties. The investigation documented more than 80 corrupt payments ranging from a $50 fee for renovations to a single family house to $20,000 for the issuance of a C of O for a commercial building. A portion of the money extorted by field inspectors was "kickedback" to DOB supervisors who controlled building inspection assignments and signed off on the issuance of C of O's.

Following the arrests, DOI's Corruption Prevention and Management Review Bureau issued a report that made twenty recommendations to DOB to correct problems in the supervision and performance of inspections, and the process of granting C of O's. DOB has taken action to address the serious corruption problem in its inspectional ranks.

TAXI INSPECTIONS ("THIRTY-NINE")

In July 1991, the Chief Supervising Inspector, four supervisors and twenty-two city taxi inspectors—more than half the inspectional force at the Taxi and Limousine Commission's Safety and Emissions Division facility in Woodside, Queens—were arrested for receiving bribes to overlook violations in yellow cabs or to allow cabs to pass inspection sight unseen. In November 1992 and July 1993, three more individuals were arrested, bringing the total to 30; and twenty-eight individuals have pled guilty.

Medallion taxi cabs are inspected three times per year to check wheel alignments, brakes, emissions, lights and other safety features. Failure to pass inspection may result in suspension of the taxi cab's medallion, currently valued at approximately $140,000. The arrested inspectors, who were paid $50 to $100 per cab, devised methods of evading or disabling tests to allow taxis to pass portions of the inspection the vehicle may not have otherwise passed. They received as much as $500 cash per week, doubling their base salary of $24,000 per year.

Following the investigation, the Mayor appointed an advisory committee to recommend changes at the testing facility, including exploring the installation of tamper-resistant equipment and improving managerial and supervisory training.

PLUMBING INSPECTORS ("MOTOWN")

Upon receiving allegations of bribery by plumbing inspectors employed by the Department of Buildings, DOI began an investigation which led to an indictment, in September 1993, of 23 active and retired inspectors by Manhattan District Attorney Robert Morgenthau. The inspectors, including the chief plumbing inspectors for Manhattan, Queens and Brooklyn, were charged with extorting dozens of payoffs—at work sites such as Police Headquarters and the World Trade Center—ranging from $50-$1000 from plumbing contractors in return for expediting inspections and speeding approvals.

Plumbing inspectors are responsible for insuring that gas lines, pipes and sprinklers are safe in renovated and newly constructed buildings. While there was no evidence inspectors overlooked safety issues or code violations, contractors paid the bribes to avoid costly delays associated with setting up appointments with inspectors and "misplaced" paper work.

The DOB implemented a new computerized management system which schedules all appointments with inspectors within three days and requires the entry of all paperwork in the computer. In addition, Mayor Dinkins proposed legislation to delegate plumbing inspection responsibilities to a private entity controlled by a board composed of a majority of city officials and to allow homeowners to have their own architects and engineers conduct plumbing inspections.

SANITATION ENFORCEMENT AGENTS ("MEAL TICKET")

In October 1993, eight Sanitation Enforcement Agents were arrested on charges of extortion and bribe receiving. SEA's are responsible for enforcing city regulations against littering and other sidewalk obstructions by issuing notices of violations to merchants and building owners who violate the regulations. Fines range from $50 to $250.

The agents, including a supervising lieutenant and three sergeants, demanded cash, meals and other gifts by promising to overlook violations or threatened to issue summonses for nonexistent infractions. The agents supplemented their city salaries by as much as $10,000 per year. The October arrests followed earlier arrests of two SEA's assigned to the same unit. One individual was arrested after evidence was developed to include weapons and narcotics sales and possession. A second SEA pled guilty to bribe receiving and was sentenced up to to four years.

TRAFFIC ENFORCEMENT AGENTS ("UPS")

In 1990, DOI received a complaint from United Parcel Service that Traffic Enforcement Agents employed by the Department of Transportation were fraudulently writing traffic tickets that were submitted to the Parking Violations Bureau but never given to

UPS drivers or placed on UPS trucks. DOI's investigation discovered more than ten TEAs who were improperly writing tickets while "cooping" in coffee shops and other places. The investigation also determined that some UPS drivers threw away valid tickets placed on the windshields of their trucks. DOI made several recommendations, which DOT has accepted, to deter cooping and the improper writing of tickets. In particular, DOT will require supervisors to make more unannounced checks on TEAs on route, a measure which will not strain existing resources.

PVB AND OTHER AGENCY SUMMONSES ("ROCKIN ROBIN"; "T. JONES"; "HERE TODAY"; "TICKETRON")

DOI has conducted several investigations prompted by its receipt of information concerning the illegal dismissal of summonses. In 1992, DOI arrested: two employees of the Department of Transportation's Parking Violations Bureau for accepting bribes to illegally dismiss hundreds of summonses valued at more than $68,000 over a seven and eight-month period, respectively; an employee of the Department of Consumer Affairs on charges that he accepted bribes to dismiss summonses against merchants who operate unlicensed video games; and a Sanitation enforcement officer on charges that he removed and destroyed at least 574 summonses issued to merchants for code violations, resulting in a minimum of $99,300 in lost revenue to the city.

Except in the case of the sanitation enforcement officer, summonses were illegally dismissed through agency computer terminals. DOI has recommended ways to tighten systems controls to prevent the illegal dismissal of summonses at PVB and the other agencies where corruption was discovered. The recommendations include more than fifty made in a report issued in August 1990 by DOI's Corruption Prevention and Management Review Bureau concerning STARS, PVB's computer system for recording and tracking summonses.

Correctional Services

The Department of Correction operates the largest municipal jail system in the United States. In Fiscal Year 1993, DOC's expense budget was $761 million, ranking it third among all city departments, after the Department of Social Services and the Police Department. DOC has an average daily prison population exceeding 18,500. It employs approximately 13,500 persons, 11,300 of whom are uniformed correction officers. The ratio of the inmate population to uniformed personnel is 1.8 to 1, the highest of any major prison system. To handle a more than doubling of the prison population in the past ten years, the number of correction officers (5400 in 1983) has more than doubled and DOC's budget ($217 million in 1983) has tripled. DOC has spent about $1.3 billion since 1985 on a major jail expansion program.

In addition to the typical corruption risks present in any large agency with substantial operating and capital budgets, DOC faces the continuing problem of the smuggling of weapons and drugs into the jails by uniformed and civilian personnel. DOI's Correctional Services Unit conducts a wide range of investigations into the operations of DOC and the conduct of DOC personnel. The unit's work includes cases leading to the arrests of correction officers for smuggling or attempting to smuggle contraband and the issuance of three major reports, two of which describe significant breakdowns in the supervision of uniformed personnel in connection with a inmate riot at a Rikers Island jail and the housing of new inmates, and the third (summarized above) discussing violations of city procurement regulations in the award of the contract for an electronic monitoring system.

INMATE DISTURBANCE ON RIKERS ISLAND ("RIKERS")

In August 1990, inmates at the Otis Bantum Correctional Facility on Rikers Island rioted after a 36-hour job action by correction officers that shut off access to the island by road and severely disrupted jail services. In 1991, DOI released a 271-page report, "The Disturbance at the Otis Bantum Correctional Center, August 14, 1990: Its Causes and the Department of Correction Response," that provided a detailed account of the riot and its causes. DOI found that the Department of Correction failed to follow its own emergency plans when responding to the riot. As a result there was a breakdown in command structure and discipline, and a substantial number of correction officers used excessive force against inmates, some of whom suffered head injuries.

DOI made a number of recommendations, which included the mobilization of the Emergency Response Unit reacting to all significant inmate disturbances; the recording of names and assignments of all correction personnel responding to an emergency; and the submission of detailed written reports by correction personnel responding to an emergency. In response, the Department of Correction issued a new emergency preparedness plan and placed new markings on protective equipment used during riots so that correction officers can be easily identified.

CONTRABAND IN CITY JAILS ("SMUGGLERS BLUE")

DOI's Office of the Inspector General for the Department of Correction has conducted investigations resulting in the arrests of more than 23 employees and contract workers of the Department of Correction for attempting to smuggle drugs, weapons and other contraband into city jails. Twenty employees—including ten correction officers, six civilian employees and four hospital workers —were arrested for attempting to smuggle cocaine and other contraband in exchange for cash to inmates at several detention facilities. In addition, three correction employees, including two correction officers, were arrested for attempting to smuggle loaded firearms to inmates, and a correction officer was arrested for having himself shot to cover up his role in a gun-smuggling scheme by two inmates.

Based on DOI's recommendation, the Department of Correction now requires all correction officers and other employees to pass through metal detectors when entering the jails to deter attempts to smuggle weapons.

24-HOUR HOUSING MANDATE ("24 HOUR")

In April 1992, DOI issued a report, "An Investigation into the Process of Admitting Inmates at the Manhattan Detention Center Complex: Violations of Department of Correction Directives and Federal Court Orders", which revealed that Department of Correction officials repeatedly violated a Federal Court order and DOC directives concerning the placement of newly admitted inmates. The Department of Correction issued a series of directives that required correction officers to record the actual times inmates are taken into custody and assigned beds after the agency was held in contempt, in November 1990, for violating a Court order that newly admitted inmates be placed in a housing area within 24 hours after DOC assumes custody.

For a two and one-half month period, January 1, 1991 through March 17, 1991, DOI's Inspector General for DOC examined admission records at the Manhattan Complex and found false entries of housing times in Correction logbooks, inaccurate housing admission times, altered entries and the failure to log inmates in DOC's computer tracking system. The report concluded that some of the abuses were the result of DOC supervisors who consciously disregarded the directives by directing that false housing times be recorded to conceal the fact that inmates were not housed within 24 hours. The report recommended that DOC pursue disciplinary action against those supervisors and correction officers involved and conduct routine audits to verify custody times.

Other Investigations and Reports

FULTON FISH MARKET ("STINGRAY")

In April 1992, DOI released its findings after a two-year under-cover investigation of the Fulton Fish Market, the center of New York's multi-million dollar wholesale seafood industry. By placing undercover agents as truckers, journeymen and retailers, DOI's investigation uncovered evidence of criminal activity including extortion, loansharking, insurance fraud and intimidation of suppliers and wholesalers. The investigation focused predominately on the "unloading crew" at the market.

Undercover investigators found that trucks delivering seafood at the market were required to wait to be unloaded by one of six unloading crews allocated to them. Wholesalers who attempted to circumvent the rules typically found that their seafood, a perishable commodity, was either unloaded last or stolen. Investigators also found that loaders made up to $200 extra per night by illegally charging a fee to retailers who parked their vehicles on public streets near the market. If retailers refused to pay, their vehicles were vandalized and property stolen.

Following the release of the report, Mayor Dinkins directed the city Department of Business Services to develop measures to strengthen enforcement, increase revenues and improve the business environment. Up to 20 additional market managers and inspectors have been hired to accomplish these proposals.

SALE OF ILLEGAL FIREARMS

During the Fulton Fish Market investigation, a DOI undercover investigator was approached by a worker at the market, advising him that if he was interested in purchasing a gun, he should see an individual named "Sally". Over the course of the next seven months, DOI purchased 37 firearms, ranging from an Uzi .9mm semiautomatic handgun, an Intratec semi-automatic machine pistol and a 12 gauge "streetsweeper" shotgun. Salvatore Fianchino was arrested in April 1991 on multiple charges involving the illegal sale and distribution of firearms, and money laundering in connection with the belief that the weapons sold were used in an illegal gambling operation. With one exception, the weapons purchased by the undercover operative had their identifying serial numbers defaced and obliterated prior to delivery.

Investigators traced some of the guns to John Zodda, a federally licensed firearms dealer, who has been described by law enforcement authorities as one of the largest single gun traffickers ever arrested in New York. In November 1992, Zodda was convicted on eight counts and sentenced to 30 months in federal prison.

DOT MAINTENANCE YARD ("HIGHWAY ROBBERY")

In November 1993, following an investigation into allegations of corruption and misconduct at the DOT Bureau of Highways' Flatlands Avenue Yard in Brooklyn, eight employees, including the Borough Supervisor in charge of the yard, were arrested on charges of theft of equipment and materials and submitting falsified time records. The arrests coincided with the release of a 32-page report detailing thefts (including a paving roller and asphalt spreader and paving materials), flagrant misuse of tens of thousands of dollars in toll tokens and tickets, performing private paving jobs on city time—even earning overtime for the hours spent on the private work—inadequate security at the yard, and the lack of inventory controls over the more than $21 million worth of materials and equipment stored at the yard.

The Flatlands Avenue Yard is responsible for all street repair and repaving in Brooklyn. The report, which concluded that the yard operated like an independent fiefdom, contains 36 recommendations for corrective action in the areas of inventory control and management, control over leave and time and control over disbursement of toll tokens and tickets.

SECURITY AND CONTROL DEFICIENCIES AT PIER 76 ("TOW POUND")

A 75-page study of the operation and security of private property, at the Department of Transportation's tow pound, located on 12th Avenue between 34th and 38th Streets in Manhattan, was issued in February 1993. One hundred thousand cars are towed annually to Pier 76, the city's largest vehicle storage and redemption center. The study found a series of problems, including unmonitored surveillance, defective perimeter fencing, inadequate lighting and a deficient data information system.

Images from 12 closed circuit cameras, installed to deter theft, were projected to an empty, and even locked room. The defective perimeter fencing, where metal ties that bind the fencing to vertical and bottom horizontal metal poles were missing in many areas, allowed unrestricted access to all areas of the pound. Lights in crucial areas throughout the pound were not repaired or replaced, and in one month during the study, 300 bulbs in the 1200 light fixtures needed to be replaced. Inaccurate and incomplete data was entered into the automated Tow Pound Information System, which keeps track of vehicles stored at the pound, creating a risk that vehicles not entered into the system may be released after the payment of a bribe.

DOI made 35 recommendations for corrective action and DOT has implemented most of them.

DOI CASES

BY HOME DEPARTMENT OF PERP*

EACH CASE IS PRECEDED BY CASE NAME AND FOLLOWED, IN PARENTHESES, BY CHARGES AND PROSECUTING AGENCY INVOLVED.

Department of Buildings

JERICO. Twenty-seven inspectors in DOB's Construction Division convicted of extorting more than $150,000 from building owners, contractors, engineers and architects in exchange for approving Certificates of Occupancy. (Extortion/U.S. Attorney for the Eastern District of New York)

MOTOWN. Twenty-three active and retired DOB plumbing inspectors arrested for accepting bribes from contractors seeking to obtain inspection "sign offs" at building sites prior to issuance of Certificates of Occupancy. (Grand Larceny/Manhattan DA)

SOCIAL CLUBS. Construction inspector solicited a bribe from undercover investigator to overlook code violations at a social club. (Bribe Receiving/Manhattan DA)

---

*From DOI 1990–1993 report to the Mayor

A.S.A.P. Employee of a waterproofing company possessed a counterfeit Special Riggers License. (Criminal Possession of a Forged Instrument/Brooklyn DA)

PALASKI PAYOFF. Building owner bribed undercover building inspector to not issue a summons for violating a Certificate of Occupancy. (Bribery/SI DA)

PING-PONG. Restaurant owner bribed undercover investigator to not issue a summons for violating Landmarks Preservation Commission regulations. (Bribery/Manhattan DA)

BQE PAYOFF. Restaurant owner bribed undercover buildings inspector to not issue a violation summons. (Bribery/Queens DA)

Department of Consumer Affairs

WHERE'S THE BEEF? Twenty managers and owners of supermarkets paid bribes to undercover agents posing as DCA weights and measures inspectors not to write violations for "short-weighted" meats. (Bribery/Bronx DA; Brooklyn DA; Queens DA; Manhattan DA)

CONSULTANTS. Private consultants paid a bribe to undercover investigator posing as DCA official to obtain licenses and have summonses deleted from city records. (Bribery/Manhattan DA)

VENDORS. Two individuals submitted forged documents to DCA to obtain preferred general vendors licenses. (Criminal Possession of a Forged Instrument/Manhattan DA)

ONE-ARMED BANDIT. Restaurant owner paid a bribe to undercover DCA inspector to not issue summonses. (Bribery/Manhattan DA)

HERE TODAY. DCA settlement officer accepted bribes to dismiss summonses issued to merchants who operate unlicensed video games. (Grand Larceny/Manhattan DA)

EASY MONEY. Two DCA employees forged and negotiated U. S. postal money orders originally submitted to DCA by license applicants for fingerprint processing fees. (Forgery/Manhattan DA.)

POSTAL ORDERS. Two DCA employees misappropriated U.S. Postal money orders purchased by the agency to pay vendor debts. (Petit Larceny/Manhattan DA)

Department of Correction

KICKBACK I. DOC assistant commissioner charged with soliciting and accepting more than $24,000 in kickbacks in exchange for steering DOC contracts to a cleaning supply company. (Extortion/U.S. Attorney for the Eastern District of New York.)

KICKBACK II. Correction officer charged with accepting payments from a janitorial supply company (Mail Fraud/U. S. Attorney for the Eastern District of New York.)

SMUGGLERS BLUE I. Nine DOC employees, including three correction officers, three hospital workers, two civilian cooks and an office aide arrested for accepting bribes to smuggle cocaine to inmates in six detention facilities. (Attempted Criminal Sale of Controlled Substance; Bribe Receiving/Manhattan DA; Bronx DA)

SMUGGLERS BLUE II. Correction Officer attempted to smuggle narcotics to an inmate at a Rikers Island facility. (Promoting Prison Contraband/Bronx DA)

SMUGGLER'S BLUE III. Correction counselor attempted to smuggle cocaine and loaded firearm to inmate after accepting a bribe from undercover investigator. (Attempted Criminal Sale of Controlled Substance/Bronx DA)

SMUGGLERS BLUE IV. Three correction officers and civilian cook arrested on charges of accepting bribes to smuggle drugs into five detention facilities. (Attempted Criminal Sale of Controlled Substance/Queens DA; Bronx DA)

SMUGGLER'S BLUE V. Montefiore Hospital worker and correction counselor arrested for smuggling razor blades to inmate on Rikers Island. (Promoting Prison Contraband/Bronx DA)

SMUGGLER'S BLUE VI. Correction officer arrested for smuggling narcotics and a loaded firearm to inmates at a Rikers Island facility. (Attempted Criminal Sale of Controlled Substance; Bribe Receiving/Bronx DA)

SMUGGLER'S BLUE VII. Correction Officer and Rikers Island cook arrested for accepting bribes to smuggle drugs to inmates. (Attempted Criminal Sale of Controlled Substance; Bribe Receiving/Bronx DA)

SMUGGLER'S BLUE VIII. Correction officer arrested for accepting a bribe to smuggle cocaine to an inmate at a Rikers Island facility. (Attempted Criminal Sale of Controlled Substance; Bribe Receiving/Bronx DA)

SMUGGLER'S BLUE IX. Correction officer arrested for accepting bribes to smuggle cocaine to inmates on Rikers Island) (Attempted Criminal Sale of a Controlled Substance; Bribe Receiving/Bronx DA)

SMUGGLER'S BLUE X. Correction Officer arrested for smuggling a gun into a Riker's Island facility that was later used to shoot another correction officer following a purported fight between inmates. (Promotion of Prison Contraband; Bribe Receiving/Bronx DA)

SMUGGLER'S BLUE XI. Correction Officer charged with arranging for two inmates to shoot him in the thigh to cover up his role in hiding a gun smuggled into Rikers by another correction officer for the inmates. (Promotion of Prison Contraband/Bronx DA)

ESCAPE. Correction officer arrested for attempting to effect escape of female inmate on Rikers Island. (Attempted Escape; Conspiracy/Bronx DA)

LOANSHARKING. DOC captain engaged in loansharking scheme by collecting 800% interest on a $5000 loan. (Criminal Usury/Queens DA)

BOGUS DOCUMENTS. DOC assistant commissioner submitted documents to the City containing false information regarding residency and background. (Forgery; Perjury/Manhattan DA)

BEATING. Rikers Island drug counselor charged with paying undercover investigator to have his ex-wife beaten. (Conspiracy; Attempted Assault/Bronx DA)

BOOKMAKERS. Two correction officers placed bets with bookmakers through an inmate incarcerated at Brooklyn House of Detention for Men. (Official Misconduct/Brooklyn DA)

Community Development Agency

NOT-FOR PROFIT I. Two employees of a not-for-profit organization defrauded the City of $26,000 by collecting simultaneous salaries as full and part-time officers of three separate programs funded by three different City agencies. (Grand Larceny/Bronx DA)

NOT-FOR-PROFIT II. Executive of a not-for-profit agency funded by the City misappropriated CDA funds. (Grand Larceny/Bronx DA)

NOT-FOR PROFIT III. Board chairman and employee of CDA-funded community-based organization misappropriated CDA funds. (Grand Larceny/Brooklyn DA)

NO WORK I. Executive director of CDA-funded program fraudulently received compensation for work not performed. (Grand Larceny/Brooklyn DA)

NO WORK II. Member of a CDA policy board submitted altered invoices to CDA requesting payment for services not actually rendered. (Forgery; Official Misconduct/Brooklyn DA)

HEAP. Individual fraudulently obtained and negotiated a HEAP support check. (Grand Larceny/Manhattan DA)

Department of Cultural Affairs

NOT-FOR PROFIT I. Deputy director of a city-funded arts center misappropriated more than $62,000 from the center. (Grand Larceny/Queens DA)

Department of Employment

EMBEZZLEMENT. Assistant Commissioner of DOE and Chairperson of a not-for-profit organization receiving city, state and federal funds charged with embezzling more than $181,000 from the organization. (Theft From Program Receiving Federal Funds/U.S. Attorney for the Eastern District of New York)

SBA. Two employees of the Small Business Association forged and submitted false documents to DOE to obtain $60,000 in city funding. (Forgery/Manhattan DA)

YMCA. Former counselor at a YMCA misappropriated city funds. (Grand Larceny/Brooklyn DA)

WELFARE I. Former Department of Employment supervisor forged and falsified employment applications to the City enabling her to collect public assistance while collecting her regular salary. (Forgery/Brooklyn DA)

WELFARE II. A DOE Human Resources specialist fraudulently received more than $27,000 in public assistance benefits and submitted falsified employment applications to the City. (Grand Larceny/Brooklyn DA)

COPY MACHINES. President of a company selling copy machines submitted forged and fraudulent bids to DOE. (Forgery; Perjury/Manhattan DA)

NOT-FOR-PROFIT. Former program director at a not-for-profit organization misappropriated City funds by submitting falsified vouchers containing forged documents. (Grand Larceny; Forgery/Bronx DA)

JIPA. Two former employees of an agency under contract with DOE to provide job training and placement submitted falsified and forged documents. (Theft From Program Receiving Federal Funds; Mail Fraud/U.S. Attorney for Eastern District of New York)

Department of Environmental Protection

VANGUARD. Four executives of a water meter services company indicted on charges of violating city contract provisions by underpaying prevailing wages, totaling more than $2.4 million, to employees installing water meters. (Grand Larceny; Conspiracy/Manhattan DA)

RIGID I. President of electrical contracting firm defrauded the city of $57,000 by submitting 17 forged supplier invoices to DEP. (Grand Larceny/Manhattan DA)

RIGID II. President of an electrical contracting firm located in Westchester County submitted false invoices to DEP in an attempt to defraud the City as to how much the company paid for its electrical supplies. (Offering a False Instrument for Filing/Westchester DA)

DOUBLE TAKE I. Two contractors paid bribes to undercover agent posing as a DEP asbestos-control inspector to remove a violation their firm received for employing an unlicensed asbestos handler. (Bribery/Bronx DA)

DOUBLE TAKE II. Official of an asbestos removal company bribed undercover agent posing as a DEP asbestos control inspector to not issue a violation. (Bribery/SI DA)

DOUBLE TAKE III. DEP employee solicited a bribe from an undercover police officer in exchange for providing confidential DEP asbestos licensing records. (Bribe Receiving/Queens DA)

INVISIBLE INK. Two DEP employees solicited kickbacks from an undercover office supply company for allowing it to submit phony billings to the agency. (Conspiracy; Mail Fraud/U.S. Attorney for the Southern District of New York)

MIDAS TOUCH. DEP supervisor directed subordinates to pour hundreds of gallons of battery acid into the NYC sewer system. (Endangering Public Health/State Attorney General)

BUS SERVICE. Bus company illegally dumped anti-freeze fluid, which drained into sewers and the Hutchinson River. (Violation of Clean Air Act/U.S. Attorney for the Southern District of New York)

PAINT DRUMS. Owner of paint company illegally stored paint-waste drums which leaked hazardous wastes. (Illegal Storage of Hazardous Waste/U.S. Attorney for the Southern District of New York)

CRUISE. Cruise boats discharged raw sewage waste into the Hudson River and New York Harbor. (Prohibition Against Pollution of Waters; Restrictions on Discharge of Sewage/Manhattan DA; State Department of Environmental Conservation)

PLUMBING. Plumber paid bribes to undercover DEP water inspector to obtain approval of house connections. (Bribery/Manhattan DA)

DIRTY WATER I. Bronx grocery store owner bribed undercover water inspector to substantially reduce his water bill. (Bribery/Bronx DA)

DIRTY WATER II. Three real estate managers bribed undercover water inspectors to reduce water bills on their property. (Bribery/Bronx DA)

NAME GAME. DEP sewage treatment worker submitted false documents in order to obtain City employment. (Forgery/Manhattan DA)

BARCO I. Co-owner of restaurant bribed undercover agent posing as an air resources inspector to not issue a noise violation and to cancel existing violation. (Bribery/Manhattan DA)

BARCO II. Restaurant manager bribed undercover DEP inspector to not issue air pollution violation. (Bribery/Manhattan DA)

BARCO III. Store owner bribed undercover agent posing as a DEP inspector to not issue a violation and offered money to Environmental Control Board Administrative Law Judge following dismissal of noise pollution violation. (Bribery/Brooklyn DA)

PETTY CASH. DEP employee misappropriated agency funds. (Petit Larceny/Queens DA)

SCRAP. DEP employee stole city-owned copper pipe and brass fittings from his work location and sold the material to a scrap metal shop. (Petit Larceny; Criminal Possession of Stolen Property/Queens DA)

VENDOR. Food vendor offered money to Environmental Control Board Administrative Law Judge after his case had been adjourned. (Bribery/Brooklyn DA)

MORTGAGE. DEP employee prepared a fraudulent letter, using DEP letterhead, to obtain a home mortgage. (Forgery/SI DA)

Department of Finance

CPA. Certified Public Accountant offered $30,000 bribe to DOF tax auditor to exclude several hundred thousand dollars of a client's personal income tax liability. (Bribery; Mail Fraud/U.S. Attorney for the Eastern District of New York)

BIDS 'R US. Contractor submitted multiple fraudulent contract bids, including forged bid bonds, to various agencies. (Submitting False Statements; Forgery/U.S. Attorney for the Southern District of New York; Manhattan DA)

GO FLY A KITE. Inquiry into scheme to defraud by a check cashing company under contract with the city, and other clients, to provide on-site check cashing services to employees. (Wire Fraud/U.S. Attorney for the Southern District of New York)

PRIVATE EYE. Private investigator, on behalf of automobile dealership, bribed DOF auditor to postpone production of business records. (Bribery/Bronx DA)

TAXING TIME I. Individual bribed DOF fraud investigator to terminate a tax fraud investigation. (Bribery/Brooklyn DA)

TAXING TIME II. Individual bribed a DOF fraud investigator to not issue summonses for failure to have a cigarette retail license. (Bribery/Manhattan DA)

PASSAGE TO INDIA. Restaurant owner bribed DOF sales tax auditor in exchange for agreement to reduce restaurant's potential tax liability. (Bribery/Brooklyn DA)

AUDIT. Taxpayer gave unlawful gratuity to DOF auditor in response to the auditor's prior assistance with DOF paperwork involving a tax delinquency. (Unlawful Gratuity/Brooklyn DA)

ZONING. Property owner bribed undercover DOF investigator to overlook city zoning violations with respect to illegal subdivisions and rentals in his home and garage. (Bribery/Queens DA)

CHECK CASH I. Individual forged and negotiated a NYC payroll check. (Forgery; Grand Larceny/Brooklyn DA)

CHECK CASH II. Chairman of a Caribbean company fraudulently endorsed and negotiated a $33,000 NYC vendor check. (Mail Fraud/U.S. Attorney for the Southern District of New York)

CHECK CASH III. Owner of an auto leasing company fraudulently negotiated two NYC vendor checks totaling $25,000. (Grand Larceny/Bronx DA)

CHECK CASH IV. Individual fraudulently endorsed and negotiated a NYC vendor's check. (Mail Theft; Forgery/U.S. Attorney for the Southern District of New York)

BAIL REFUND I. Individual fraudulently altered a DOF bail refund check. (Forgery/Manhattan DA)

BAIL REFUND II. Individual stole and fraudulently cashed a $24,000 bail refund check. (Grand Larceny; Forgery/Brooklyn DA)

BOCCI BALL. City assessor bribed a Brooklyn homeowner to not increase the assessment on his two-family residence. (Bribery/Brooklyn DA)

PUSHERMAN. DOF supervisor charged with selling cocaine to an undercover DOI investigator. (Criminal Possession of a Controlled Substance/Manhattan DA)

RUBBER CHECK. FISA employee stole and fraudulently negotiated a sample payroll check. (Forgery/Manhattan DA)

POSTMAN. DOF office aide stole a taxpayer's money order submitted as payment for a tax stamp, which is required to legally operate taxis in the city. (Petit Larceny/Brooklyn DA)

COLD CASH CAPER. DOF intern stole cash submitted by taxpayers as payment for property tax. (Grand Larceny/Queens DA)

FALSE DOCUMENTS. Official within the DOF intentionally filed false documents with city agencies to conceal residency outside New York City. (Offering False Instrument for Filing/Manhattan DA)

LOST CHECKS. Individual fraudulently endorsed and negotiated eight NYC vendor checks stolen from an attorney representing indigent clients for the city. (Forgery/Brooklyn DA)

PAGERS. College aide in DOF's administration division stole paging devices. (Grand Larceny/Manhattan DA)

Fire Department

IMPERSONATION. Individual fraudulently cashed Fire Department payroll checks by misrepresenting his identity and possessed FDNY property without official authorization. (Forgery; Grand Larceny/Brooklyn DA)

BIG TIME. Installer of sprinkler systems bribed undercover fire inspector to obtain FDNY approval for his company to install fire suppression systems. (Bribery/Bronx DA)

GRAB BAG. Fire prevention specialist accepted unlawful gratuity during an inspection. (Receiving Unlawful Gratuity/Manhattan DA)

DEEP POCKETS. Three operators of an auto repair shop bribed undercover fire inspectors. (Bribery/Queens DA)

GREENBACKS. Business owner bribed undercover investigator to dismiss fire violations. (Bribery/Brooklyn DA)

BOMBAY GOLD. Two building owners bribed undercover investigators to overlook fire violations. (Bribery/Manhattan DA)

BIG SHOT. FDNY college intern displayed a loaded firearm after discovering cash had been stolen from her bag. (Criminal Possession of a Weapon/Brooklyn DA)

CHECK CASH. NYC firefighter stole and cashed payroll check belonging to another firefighter. (Grand Larceny/Bronx DA)

FALSE ALARM. Three firefighters submitted fraudulent claims to the FDNY in order to secure reimbursement for damage allegedly incurred to their personal auto while on duty. (Criminal Possession of Forged Instrument/Brooklyn DA)

BAND AID. Former firefighter fraudulently obtained an accidental disability pension by falsely reporting that he was injured while on duty. (Grand Larceny/Manhattan DA)

BAD MEDICINE. Manager of a Bronx pharmacy bribed an undercover investigator posing as an FDNY inspector in order to obtain DOB Equipment Use Permit to operate an air conditioning system. (Bribery/Bronx DA)

Department of General Services

DOUBLE INDEMNITY I. General manager of waterproofing and restoration company and president of surety company prepared fraudulent surety bonds for construction contracts with city, state and federal governments. (Mail Wire Fraud/U.S. Attorney for the Southern District of New York)

DOUBLE INDEMNITY II. President of a maintenance company submitted false surety bonds for various construction and maintenance contracts with the city and state. (Wire Fraud/U.S. Attorney for the Southern District of New York)

DOUBLE INDEMNITY III. Contracting company submitted fraudulent surety bonds on various city, state and federal construction projects. (Mail Fraud/U.S. Attorney for the Southern District of New York)

OUT OF ORBIT. Contractor submitted fraudulent surety bonds on various city, state and federal construction projects. (Conspiracy/U.S. Attorney for the Southern District of New York)

PREVAILING WAGE I. Waterproofing company and its president violated prevailing wage law and submitted falsified certified payroll reports to numerous city agencies. (Grand Larceny/Manhattan DA)

PREVAILING WAGE II. Company president violated prevailing wage law and submitted falsified certified payroll reports to numerous City agencies. (Grand Larceny/Manhattan DA)

TALK IS CHEAP. Two DGS watchmen and seven non-city employees, acting in concert with others, placed thousands of dollars in unauthorized overseas telephone calls by tampering with a switchboard in a city-owned building. (Theft of Services; Commercial Bribe Receiving/Manhattan DA)

SCRAP METAL. DGS employee stole city-owned property and attempted to sell it to a scrap metal dealer. (Petit Larceny/Brooklyn DA)

TIP IN. DGS office aide stole 203 electronic digital paging devices by placing forged purchase orders on behalf of DGS. (Grand Larceny/Manhattan DA)

CHEAP BEEP. DGS administrative supervisor forged a NYC purchase requisition to obtain property for personal use. (Forgery/Manhattan DA)

CITY LEASE. DGS staff analyst defrauded a prospective lessee of city-owned property by improperly taking purported rent payments. (Grand Larceny/Manhattan DA)

TIMBER. Businessman fraudulently converted city-owned property for personal gain and unlawfully collected $17,600 in rents. (Grand Larceny/Queens DA)

BATES' TACKLE. DGS employee improperly disposed of City supplies and submitted delivery invoices falsely claiming the supplies were delivered to other city agencies. (Grand Larceny; Forgery/Queens DA)

BORO HALL. Company under contract with DGS submitted false invoices totaling more than $72,000. (Grand Larceny/Manhattan DA)

SHORTCHANGE. Company with whom DGS contracted to remove scrap metal defrauded city by intentionally understating gross weight of vehicles used to transport the loads. (Grand Larceny/Manhattan DA)

HPPT. Twenty-two DGS and DOS employees falsified employment applications by fraudulently claiming prior work experience to qualify for the title of High Pressure Plant Tender. (Offering False Instrument for Filing/Manhattan DA)

PARK AT YOUR OWN RISK. Individual posing as a DGS employee participated in a scheme to extort $15,000 from a DGS tenant operating a parking lot in Brooklyn; and the DGS tenant, and another individual, submitted false documentation to DGS concerning his business experience. (Attempted Grand Larceny; Offering False Instrument for Filing/Brooklyn DA)

FALSETTO. President of a contracting company submitted a falsified Vendex principal questionnaire to DGS for three contracts valued at $6 million. (Offering a False Instrument for Filing; Manhattan DA)

OIL SLICK. Two executives of an oil delivery company bribed an undercover investigator to refrain from fining them for operating the company in an area zoned for residences. (Bribery/SI DA)

Department of Health

BAD CHECKS. DOH employee and two others, including HRA case worker, falsely generated more than $14,000 in emergency children's service benefits from HRA. (Grand Larceny/Manhattan DA)

PASSAGE TO INDIA. Restaurant owner bribed DOH inspector for a favorable inspection. (Bribery/Brooklyn DA)

PUPPY WORLD I. Owner of a dog grooming service bribed undercover health inspector to overlook violations. (Bribery/Brooklyn DA)

PUPPY WORLD. Stable owner bribed undercover health inspector to overlook violations. (Bribery/SI DA)

CODE VIOLATIONS I. Restaurant owner bribed undercover health inspector to overlook violations. (Bribery/Manhattan DA)

CODE VIOLATIONS II. Restaurant owner bribed undercover investigator to overlook health violations. (Bribery/Manhattan DA)

CODE VIOLATIONS III. Restaurant owner and associate paid bribes to undercover investigators to overlook health and fire code violations. (Bribery/Brooklyn DA)

IL GIORNO. Two restaurant owners bribed undercover health inspectors to overlook violations. (Bribery/Manhattan DA)

GIUSEPPE. Restaurant owner bribed undercover health inspector to overlook violations and the lack of a permit. (Bribery/Brooklyn DA)

MFV. Individual used a fraudulent social security card in applying for a license to operate a mobile food cart. (Offering False Instrument for Filing/Manhattan DA)

PASSPORT. Employee in DOH's Bureau of Vital Records forged a birth certificate to obtain a U.S. passport. (Forgery/Manhattan DA)

OH BROTHER. Individual fraudulently attempted to obtain deceased brother's birth certificate. (Offering False Instrument for Filing/Manhattan DA)

HISSBANK. DOH Special Officer stole a checkbook belonging to another DOH employee and forged four checks payable to commercial entities. (Forgery/Manhattan DA)

14 BROTHERS. Manager of a Brooklyn restaurant bribed two undercover investigators to overlook health and building violations. (Bribery/Brooklyn DA)

MFV LIST. DOH employee altered a list of applicants for mobile food vendors by inserting her son's name over another potential permit holder. (Forgery/Manhattan DA)

Housing Authority

RENT ME. Director of a Housing Authority community center accepted money to rent the center for various functions. (Grand Larceny/Brooklyn DA)

DOUBLE CHECK. Housing Authority employee fraudulently received a replacement pay check after he removed his original check from a Housing Authority office before pay day. (Petit Larceny/Manhattan DA)

PAINTING CONTRACTOR. Private painting contractor bribed a Housing Authority employee to authorize payment for the work the contractor never did. (Grand Larceny/Manhattan DA)

OVERTIME. Housing Authority computer systems manager attempted to defraud the authority by engaging in a scheme to claim, and split with, unearned overtime pay for an authority consultant. (Attempted Grand Larceny/Manhattan DA)

Housing Preservation and Development

IN-REM. Eight HPD inspectors and supervisors and six contractors arrested on charges of steering repair work in exchange for bribes amounting to a percentage of the contract price. (Bribery; Bribe Receiving/Manhattan DA)

HELTER SHELTER. Non-profit organization submitted more than $100,000 in fraudulent bills to HPD for maintenance and repair work at city-owned family shelter. (Money Laundering; Tax Evasion/U.S. Attorney for the Southern District of New York

DEEP POCKETS. Superintendents of a building maintenance company under contract with the city continued to be paid long after their buildings were redeemed by private owners. (Money Laundering/U.S. Attorney for the Southern District of New York)

HANDYMAN SPECIAL. Individual engaged in loansharking and theft of Gotham Company payroll checks. (Grand Larceny/Manhattan DA)

PROCTOR'S GAMBLE. HPD supervisor solicited bribes from job applicants in exchange for providing answers to HPD-administered exam (Bribe Receiving/Queens DA)

CAPITAL IMPROVEMENTS. Two employees in HPD's Capital Improvements Program solicited bribes from private contractors to prevent delays at project sites and provide information on HPD projects. (Bribe Receiving/Brooklyn DA)

RENT ME I. Five members of a realty company illegally rented apartments in city-owned buildings. (Grand Larceny; Forgery/Bronx DA)

RENT ME II. Superintendent illegally rented apartments in city-owned buildings (Grand Larceny/Bronx DA)

SQUATTERS. City employee illegally collected rent from squatters living in HPD residential buildings. (Scheme to Defraud/Bronx DA)

NICK. HPD inspector solicited and accepted bribe from building landlord in exchange for overlooking violations. (Bribe Receiving/Bronx DA)

PAY ME. HPD employee solicited and accepted a bribe in exchange for approving payment requests. (Bribe Receiving/Bronx DA)

CHURCH DONATIONS. Former real property manager solicited bribe to illegally rent a city-owned apartment. (Bribe Receiving/Bronx DA)

ILLEGAL CONVERSION. HPD employee bribed undercover investigator to not report illegal conversion of subject's private home. (Bribery/Queens DA)

OPERATION RERUN. Former HPD employee and associate solicited bribe in return for promise to rent vacant HPD storefront properties. (Grand Larceny/Manhattan DA)

BROOKLYN CODE. Housing inspector solicited a bribe to overlook hazardous building violations. (Bribery/Brooklyn DA)

WIRE ME. Owner of electrical contracting firm bribed undercover investigator to not file a report on electrical work performed. (Bribery/Brooklyn DA)

CONSTRUCTIVE CRITICISM I. Principals of two construction companies bribed undercover investigator to arrange full payment of invoices previously reduced or rejected for substandard work. (Bribery/Queens DA)

CONSTRUCTIVE CRITICISM II. HPD contractor bribed undercover inspector to overlook deficient work. (Bribery/SI DA)

NYCHA. Board member of the NYC Housing Authority made false statements on income affidavits submitted to the city-aided housing company managing the building where he resides and may have evaded federal taxes by failing to report income derived from the rental and sale of real property. (Tax Evasion; Filing False Statements/U.S. Attorney for the Southern District of New York; Manhattan DA)

J51. Management company submitted false documentation to facilitate J51 application. (Defrauding Government; U.S. Attorney for the Southern District of New York)

SCORPIO. Landlord bribed undercover housing inspector to dismiss pending violations on three buildings. (Bribery/Bronx DA)

KITKATZ. Landlord bribed undercover investigator posing as a housing inspector in exchange for promise to dismiss building violations. (Bribery/Queens DA)

GREENBACK. Four landlords paid bribes to undercover investigator to overlook housing code violations. (Bribery/Manhattan DA).

ILLEGAL BIDS. Construction manager for a not-for-profit community group filed false information concerning the legitimacy of bids submitted by contractors and accepted an illegal payment from one vendor to issue work to him. (Commercial Bribery/Brooklyn DA)

TENANTS ASSOCIATION. Manager of a City-owned building misappropriated money from the account of the Tenants Association and deposited rent funds into his personal bank account. (Grand Larceny/Bronx DA)

CODE VIOLATIONS I. Building owners bribed a housing inspector to overlook serious code violations existing against their building. (Bribery/Bronx DA)

CODE VIOLATIONS II. Managing agent bribed investigator/inspector to delete existing housing code violations. (Bribery/Manhattan DA)

CODE VIOLATIONS III. Owner of a residential building bribed housing inspector to delete existing code violations. (Bribery/Brooklyn DA)

CODE VIOLATIONS IV. Landlord bribed undercover investigator to delete housing code violations pending against his building. (Bribery/Brooklyn DA)

CODE VIOLATIONS V. Two building owners bribed housing inspector to delete pending housing code violations. (Bribery/Queens DA)

CODE VIOLATIONS VL. Bronx landlord bribed undercover HPD inspector to overlook existing code violations. (Bribery/Bronx DA)

CODE VIOLATIONS VII. Managing agent and landlord bribed undercover housing inspector to dismiss code violations pending against their building. (Bribery/Brooklyn DA)

CODE VIOLATIONS VIII. Landlord bribed HPD inspector and undercover investigator to overlook housing code violations. (Bribery/Queens DA)

CODE VIOLATIONS IX. Landlord bribed undercover investigator to overlook housing code violations. (Bribery/Brooklyn DA)

SRO. Individual bribed an undercover HPD inspector not to report housing violations. (Bribery/Brooklyn DA)

PAYROLL THEFT. Employee of company under contract with the city to supply superintendents and maintenance workers for city-owned residential buildings stole and negotiated a company payroll check. (Grand Larceny/Manhattan DA)

TIL PROGRAM. Acting treasurer of tenants association for a building participating in HPD's Tenant Interim Lease Program negotiated a series of forged checks drawn from the association's account. (Grand Larceny/Manhattan DA)

MATTER OF CONSCIENCE. Former treasurer of a tenants association in a City-owned building arrested for stealing rent payments submitted by the building's tenants. (Grand Larceny/Manhattan DA)

CHECK CASH. Former HPD office aide altered and negotiated four HPD money orders totaling $1420 (Grand larceny, Forgery/ManhattanDA)

Human Resources Administration/ Child Welfare Administration

BIG APPLE. Forty individuals, including eight HRA employees, as well as drivers with a car service under contract with HRA to transport abused/neglected children, involved in scheme that defrauded the agency of millions of dollars by submitting false billing vouchers. (Mail Fraud; Forgery/U.S. Attorney for the Eastern District of New York; Manhattan DA)

EHCCI. Three individuals, including former assistant director of health care service agency funded by city, charged with diverting more than $1.1 million from agency programs to their own use. (Grand Larceny; Conspiracy/Manhattan DA)

HSS/PRHASP. Three former directors of two anti-poverty programs in the Bronx charged with stealing more than $180,000 in public funds earmarked for the programs. (Theft of Public Funds; Money Laundering/U.S. Attorney for the Southern District of New York)

PAYROLL FORGERY I. Former bookkeeper of a home attendant program, funded by the city, cashed more than $34,000 in forged paychecks obtained from the program's payroll account. (Grand Larceny; Manhattan DA)

TELECOMMUNICATIONS. Four individuals involved in scheme to defraud HRA/CWA of $750,000 in long distance telephone charges by telephonically altering an exchange switch in the agency's telephone network. (Wire Fraud/U.S. Attorney for the Southern District of New York)

RYERSON. Twenty-seven HRA employees and two others participated in scheme to steal equipment and supplies from HRA warehouse and engaged in overtime fraud. (Possession of Stolen Property; Conspiracy/Brooklyn DA)

PRE-PLACEMENT. Former director of HRA's Office of Pre-Placement Services convicted of stealing city property from OPPS. (Grand Larceny/Bronx DA)

TWO-PARTY CHECKS I. Two individuals obtained more than 600 two-party rent checks, exceeding $75,000, from welfare recipients. (Interstate Transportation of Stolen Government Funds; U.S. Attorney for the Southern District of New York)

TWO-PARTY CHECKS II. Bronx store owner improperly negotiated 509 two-party public assistance checks totaling more than $100,000. (Bank Fraud; U.S . Attorney for the Southern District of New York)

TWO-PARTY CHECKS III. Market owner and three others improperly cashed 763 HRA two-party public assistance checks totaling more than $100,000. (Bank Fraud; Theft of Public Money/U.S. Attorney for the Southern District of New York)

OCSE. Twenty-five individuals, including four HRA employees, fraudulently received child support benefits from HRA Office of Child Support Enforcement (Mail Fraud; Conspiracy/U.S. Attorney for the Southern District of New York)

WELFARE I. HRA eligibility specialist solicited and received cash payments and food stamps from a public assistance recipient. (Petit Larceny; Official Misconduct/Brooklyn DA)

WELFARE II. HRA eligibility specialist charged with stealing thousands of dollars in cash and food stamps from HRA and six welfare clients. (Grand Larceny; Scheme to Defraud/ Brooklyn DA)

WELFARE III. HRA employee fraudulently diverted public assistance checks, intended for the rent of welfare recipients, to his personal bank account. (Theft From Program Receiving Federal Funds; U.S. Attorney for the Southern District of New York)

WELFARE IV. HRA eligibility specialist fraudulently obtained HRA funds. (Grand Larceny/Brooklyn DA)

WELFARE V. HRA eligibility specialist illegally obtained benefits through a fraudulent welfare scheme. (Grand Larceny; Forgery/ Brooklyn DA)

WELFARE VI. Former HRA eligibility specialist falsely generated and received public assistance benefits. (Grand Larceny; Forgery/ Brooklyn DA)

WELFARE VII. HRA eligibility specialist arranged for two relatives and an associate to fraudulently receive public assistance benefits. (Grand Larceny; Forgery/Manhattan DA)

WELFARE VIII. Assistant office manager in an HRA income maintenance center opened two public assistance cases and fraudulently generated public assistance benefits. (Grand Larceny/Brooklyn DA)

WELFARE IX. Supervisor in an HRA income support center fraudulently received public assistance, food stamps and medical assistance benefits. (Theft of Public Money/U.S. Attorney for the Southern District of New York)

WELFARE X. Two NYC employees fraudulently obtained public assistance benefits while gainfully employed. (Fraudulent Claim/U.S. Attorney for the Southern District of New York)

WELFARE XI. HRA eligibility specialist fraudulently issued food stamps to her husband and brother and her husband fraudulently applied for and received public assistance benefits. (Forgery; Grand Larceny/Queens DA)

WELFARE XII. HRA employee concealed employment in order to falsely receive public assistance and food stamp benefits. (Grand Larceny/Manhattan DA)

WELFARE XIII. Two HRA employees fraudulently caused six food stamp cases to be opened for persons not entitled to receive benefits in exchange for a kickback of the proceeds. (Grand Larceny; Tampering With Public Records/Brooklyn DA)

WELFARE XIV. HRA office aide fraudulently received public assistance and food stamp benefits for herself and three children. (Grand Larceny/Bronx DA)

AIDS FUNDS. HRA case worker misappropriated HRA funds intended to benefit AIDS clients. (Grand Larceny/Brooklyn DA)

NEVINS IMC. HRA employee forged the signature of a co-worker in order to provide an individual with documentation necessary to receive more than $16,000 in public assistance and food stamps. (Grand Larceny/Brooklyn DA)

EMERGENCY ASSISTANCE I. HRA eligibility specialist conspired with public assistance recipient in fraudulent issuance of emergency public assistance checks. (Grand Larceny/Brooklyn DA)

EMERGENCY ASSISTANCE II. HRA caseworker submitted fraudulent authorization forms thereby falsely generating emergency children's services benefits for two associates. (Grand Larceny/Brooklyn DA)

EMERGENCY ASSISTANCE III. Former HRA case worker and two public assistance recipients misappropriated emergency children's services funds. (Grand Larceny; Forgery/Bronx DA)

EMERGENCY ASSISTANCE IV. Three public assistance recipients fraudulently received emergency public assistance funds. (Grand Larceny/Brooklyn DA)

EMERGENCY ASSISTANCE V. Former public assistance recipient fraudulently received emergency rent arrears benefits. (Grand Larceny; Manhattan DA)

EMERGENCY ASSISTANCE VI. Three city employees and four public assistance recipients negotiated 29 emergency public assistance checks previously stolen from HRA. (Forgery; Grand Larceny/Manhattan DA)

FALSE IDENTITY. Former HRA temporary employee used a fraudulent identity and social security number to receive employment income and public assistance benefits. (Grand Larceny/ Brooklyn DA)

MEDICAID I. Two individuals fraudulently obtained assistance from Aid to Families With Dependent Children, Food Stamp and Medicaid programs for the poor. (Grand Larceny; Bribery/ Brooklyn DA)

MEDICAID II. HRA employee defrauded city and state of more than $86,000 by enrolling 130 fictitious and unauthorized recipients in the Medicaid program. (Criminal Possession of a Forged Instrument/Medicaid Fraud)

MISAPPROPRIATION OF FUNDS I. Bookkeeper of a city-funded organization misappropriated funds from the program and fraudulently received public assistance benefits from HRA. (Theft of Federal Funds/U.S. Attorney for the Southern District of New York)

MISAPPROPRIATION OF FUNDS II. Former bookkeeper of HRA-funded senior center misappropriated funds from the center. (Grand Larceny/Manhattan DA)

DR. GREEN DCC. Former director and bookkeeper of an HRA-funded day care center misappropriated funds by making unauthorized payments to themselves. (Grand Larceny/Bronx DA)

PAYROLL FORGERY. Former bookkeeper of HRA-funded service provider fraudulently cashed forged paychecks from the program's payroll account. (Grand Larceny/Bronx DA)

HOLLAND RFP. Community service organization submitted a fraudulent signature page with its application to operate a housing center for the city. (Forgery/Manhattan DA)

NOT-FOR-PROFIT. Executive Director of a not-for profit organization funded by the city received a second salary while concurrently employed at another city-funded program. (Grand Larceny/Manhattan DA)

GRATUITY I. HRA eligibility specialist solicited unlawful gratuity from a public assistance recipient. (Receiving Unlawful Gratuity/Manhattan DA)

GRATUITY II. HRA eligibility specialist solicited and received unlawful gratuity from public assistance recipient. (Petit Larceny; Official Misconduct/Brooklyn DA)

NO-SHOW I. Individual received a salary from HRA for a no-show job. (Mail Fraud; Theft of Public Money/U.S. Attorney for the Southern District of New York)

NO-SHOW II. HRA employee solicited bribes from another employee in return for paying the employee for time not worked. (Bribe Receiving/Manhattan DA)

RESERVES. A special officer assigned to HRA's Camp LaGuardia Mens Shelter in Orange County submitted fraudulent documents to HRA to establish that his absences from work were caused by his service as a military reservist, which would entitle him to receive his regular pay.(Grand Larceny/Orange County DA)

AWOL. Former HRA employee paid an HRA timekeeper to issue his pay checks while AWOL from his job. (Grand Larceny; Defrauding Government/Manhattan DA)

KINSHIP. HRA employee, serving as a kinship foster parent, submitted forged receipts to CWA's Division of Adoption and Foster Care Services to fraudulently seek reimbursement for expenditures, and concealed prior criminal convictions on foster parent application forms. (Offering a False Instrument for Filing/Brooklyn DA)

CITY PROPERTY. HRA employee stole city property that had been entrusted to his care and delivery. (Grand Larceny/Bronx DA)

OVERTIME. HRA employee received $51,000 in fraudulent overtime claims. (Grand Larceny/Brooklyn DA)

FALSE STATEMENTS. HRA employee made false statements in Personnel Department documents regarding criminal history and employment background. (Offering a False Instrument for Filing/Manhattan DA)

CHILD ABUSE. HRA case worker sexually molested a child during a foster care home visit. (Aggravated Sexual Abuse/Queens DA)

JUNIOR. Individual engaged in deviate sexual intercourse with an underage male. (Sodomy/Brooklyn DA)

SHELTER. HRA institutional aide stole food and supplies from family shelter. (Petit Larceny/Bronx DA)

Department of Juvenile Justice

SPOFFORD. Juvenile counselor employed by DJJ was charged with sexually abusing a 15-year-old male resident at Spofford Juvenile Center. (Sodomy/Bronx DA)

Marshal's Bureau

OPERATION PAYDIRT. City Marshal misappropriated funds from Housing Authority apartment where he was performing an eviction. (Grand Larceny; Bribery/Manhattan DA)

CREDITORS I. City Marshal misappropriated funds he was required to hold in trust for creditors who hired him to enforce civil court judgments. (Grand Larceny/Queens DA)

CREDITORS II. City Marshal misappropriated funds entrusted to him by creditors who hired him to enforce civil court judgments. (Grand Larceny/Queens DA)

CREDITORS III. City Marshal misappropriated $59,000 he collected and held for his clients. (Criminal Possession of Stolen Property/Manhattan DA)

INVISIBLE MAN. City Marshal committed perjury during DOI hearing conducted concerning an eviction he performed. (Perjury/Manhattan DA)

PAPER CHASE. Owner of a debt collection agency stole $100,000 by diverting to his own accounts checks destined for creditors with civil court judgments. (Grand Larceny; Forgery/Manhattan DA)

WATSON. Collector for a City Marshal remitted only one-third of the proceeds collected from a judgment/debtor and falsified Marshal's records to cover up theft. (Grand Larceny; Forgery/Manhattan DA)

S & T. Two individuals impersonated attorneys while attempting to make collections on behalf of collection agency. (Unauthorized Practice of Law/State Attorney General.)

Department of Mental Health, Mental Retardation and Alcoholism Services

LINCOLN HOSPITAL. Former Associate Director of Lincoln Hospital hired three per-diem employees at a total of $123,000 who, over a 15-month period, performed little or no work. (Grand Larceny; Defrauding Government/U.S. Attorney for the Southern District of New York; Bronx DA)

RESIDENCY. Assistant commissioner of DMHMRAS made false statements regarding residency in official documents filed with various agencies. (Perjury; Offering False Instrument for Filing/Manhattan DA)

BRONX COMMITTEE. Former fiscal officer of a DMHMRAS-funded program charged with stealing more than $86,000 from the program. (Grand Larceny/Bronx DA)

PAYROLL CHECK. College aide in DMHMRAS' Office of Fiscal Services stole and fraudulently negotiated a payroll check issued to a co-worker. (Forgery; Petit Larceny/Manhattan DA)

Department of Parks and Recreation

ASP. DPR employee accepted payments from defendants to avoid performing maintenance duties in the city's parks under the Alternative Sentencing Program. (Bribe Receiving; Official Misconduct/Manhattan DA)

HOT ROCKS. Individual illegally purchased cobblestones stolen from the city. (Attempted Criminal Possession of Stolen Property/Bronx DA)

DEPOSIT. Former DPR employee stole and negotiated a concessionaire's security deposit refund check. (Grand Larceny; Forgery/Manhattan DA)

PAPA. DPR employee fraudulently cashed a payroll check issued to another DPR employee. (Grand Larceny; Possession of Stolen Property/Manhattan DA)

LITCHFIELD MANSION. DPR employee stole and fraudulently negotiated a payroll check issued to another DPR employee. (Petit Larceny/Brooklyn DA)

LIBERTY. DPR enforcement patrol officer used excessive force during arrest of an unlicensed vendor. (Assault; Official Misconduct/Manhattan DA)

FALSE NOTES. Former DPR lifeguard submitted forged doctors' notes and falsified DPR leave-usage forms to account for absences from work. (Forgery/Queens DA)

DOUBLE TALK. DPR employee sold stolen city-owned equipment. (Criminal Possession of Stolen Property/Brooklyn DA)

FENCES. Contractor submitted a fraudulent Vendex questionnaire to DPR and attempted to coerce a DPR employee to approve a payment voucher for unauthorized work. (Perjury; Attempted Coercion/Queens DA)

CORPORAL. Construction company, and its current and former president, submitted a fraudulent bid bond to DPR in order to secure a $1.1 million construction contract. (Offering a False Instrument for Filing/Queens DA)

Department of Personnel

TA/PD. Certain police officers obtained exam questions in advance of taking of promotional exam from a police lieutenant who participated in writing the exam. (Grand Larceny; Perjury/Manhattan DA)

RIGGERS LICENSE. Employee of a waterproofing company submitted falsified documents in connection with a Special Riggers License exam administered by the Department of Personnel. (Forgery/Manhattan DA)

Department of Ports and Trade

FERRY PASSES. DPT assistant commissioner solicited and accepted ferry passes from a DPT licensee. (Bribe Receiving/Manhattan DA)

CARPARK. Officials of a company bidding on a contract with the city submitted a disclosure statement to DPT containing false information about the financial condition of the company. (Offering a False Instrument for Filing/ManhattanDA)

Department of Probation

DRUG TEST. Lab helper in the Department of Probation's substance abuse and verification program solicited and accepted payment to provide "clean" urine sample for testing the presence of drugs.(Bribe Receiving/Brooklyn DA)

BROTHER. Individual gave an unlawful gratuity to her brother's probation officer. (Unlawful Gratuity/SI DA)

Public Administrator's Office

SOCIAL SECURITY. Office aide in Public Administrator's Office fraudulently endorsed and cashed social security checks of decedents. (Embezzling Public Funds/U.S. Attorney for the Southern District of New York.)

Department of Sanitation

NEEDLES. Eight physicians and staff members made monthly payments to sanitation worker and undercover investigator to remove medical and trade waste from medical offices, clinics, etc. (Bribery/Manhattan DA)

TRANSBORO. Owner of a waste hauling company made two illegal payments to Sanitation police officer to inform him whenever his company's activities were under surveillance. (Bribery/Brooklyn DA)

BARGE TOW. President of an unlicensed insurance company issued fraudulent performance bond for submission to DOS to secure a city contract. (Grand Larceny/Manhattan DA)

HUNTSBULK. City sanitation worker solicited and received five illegal payments from undercover investigators in exchange for allowing the improper disposal of commercial waste. (Bribe Receiving/Bronx DA)

VNB. DOS payroll supervisor fraudulently obtained 284 Verrazano Narrows Bridge tokens by submitting falsified toll receipts to DOS. (Grand Larceny/Queens DA)

DVO. Two sanitation workers misappropriated a privately-owned flatbed truck and falsified DOS records to conceal the theft. (Grand Larceny; Falsifying Business Records/Brooklyn DA)

JAWS. DOS auto mechanic conducted loansharking operation at DOS Central Repair shop. (Usury/Queens DA)

COLONEL. DOS employee accepted unlawful payments in exchange for moving commercial waste DOS workers are prohibited from taking. (Bribe Receiving/Bronx DA)

BEACHBOYS. Two DOS employees accepted unlawful payments in exchange for removing commercial waste DOS workers are prohibited from taking. (Bribe Receiving/Brooklyn DA)

BBM CHECKS. DOS employee fraudulently cashed three other DOS employees' paychecks. (Grand Larceny/SI DA)

PENSION. DOS employee and associate stole and negotiated eight DOS pension checks. (Grand Larceny/Manhattan DA)

MERCHANTS I. Manager of a clinical lab made two illegal payments to a Sanitation Enforcement Agent and undercover DOI investigator to avoid being issued summonses. (Bribery/Brooklyn DA)

MERCHANTS II. Proprietor of a fruit and vegetable store made four illegal payments to Sanitation Enforcement Agents to overlook violations. (Bribery/Manhattan DA)

MERCHANTS LLI. Green grocers made seven illegal payments to Sanitation Enforcement Agents and undercover investigators to avoid receiving summonses. (Bribery/Brooklyn DA)

LOANSHARK. Two sanitation workers charged a co-worker, to whom they lent money, usurious interest rates. (Grand Larceny/Brooklyn DA)

PAPER CUT. Three Brooklyn-based paper recycling companies stole recyclable paper and DOS recyclable paper bins from DOS and one of its contractors. (Grand Larceny/Brooklyn DA)

Special Assignments/Economic Development

STINGRAY. Investigation into activities at the Fulton Fish Market, including extortion, loansharking, illegal sale of firearms. (Illegal Sale/Purchase of Firearms; Mail Fraud; Money Laundering/U.S. Attorney for the Southern District of New York)

NYCERS. Individual defrauded New York City Employees Retirement System by continuing to cash his deceased father's pension checks. (Grand Larceny/Manhattan DA)

HOVERSPEED. Private consultant extorted money from a ferry service company in connection with its application for a grant with the Economic Development Corporation. (Hobbs Act/U.S. Attorney for the Southern District of New York)

LAGUARDIA. President and supervisor of cleaning service company offered monthly payments to LaGuardia Community College official to quash complaints about the firm's performance on its $700,000/year contract. (Bribery; Conspiracy/Queens DA)

KEIWAT. Construction company submitted sworn proposer's qualification application containing false information in effort to obtain contracts with two city agencies. (Offering False Instrument for Filing/Manhattan DA)

CUNY. Individual unlawfully obtained funds by submitting forged personnel action forms and time records to City University of New York Research Foundation. (Grand Larceny; Forgery/Manhattan DA)

HUNTER. Former Hunter College student solicited and accepted cash from 10 students in exchange for arranging for their grades to be changed in the college's computers. (Computer Tampering; Falsifying Business Records/Manhattan DA)

CCNY. Former employee of City College of New York forged time records and continued to receive a salary during a period when she was no longer employed. (Grand Larceny; Forgery/Manhattan DA)

ELECTIONS. Board of Elections officer fraudulently acquired and cashed 11 payroll checks. (Grand Larceny; Forgery/Manhattan DA)

LAW DEPARTMENT. Former Law Department employee stole paychecks belonging to several Law Department attorneys. (Grand Larceny; Forgery/Manhattan DA)

KINGSBOROUGH. Former security guard at Kingsborough Community College of the City University of New York stole blank checks and harassed a professor. (Grand Larceny; Forgery/Brooklyn DA)

COMPUTER. Office aide in facilities management in the Mayor's Office attempted to steal a computer monitor from a city office.

(Attempted Petit Larceny/Manhattan DA)

HEALTH KICK. Four city employees and a former employee of General Health Incorporated defrauded GHI of $115,000 by submitting false claims. (Mail Fraud/U.S. Attorney for the Southern District of New York)

RING. City employee stole personal property belonging to a co-worker. (Grand Larceny/Manhattan DA)

Taxi and Limousine Commission

THIRTY-NINE. Thirty inspectors in the TLC Safety and Emissions Division arrested on charges of receiving bribes to overlook violations in yellow cabs or to allow cabs to pass inspections sight unseen. (Extortion/U.S. Attorney for the Eastern District of New York)

TAXI I. Medallion cab driver offered bribe to TLC inspector to not issue violations summonses. (Bribery/Manhattan DA)

TAXI II. Livery cab driver offered unlawful payment to Administrative Law Judge in exchange for dismissing two TLC summonses. (Bribery/Manhattan DA)

TAXI III. Taxi license applicant attempted to bribe testgiver in order to obtain a license. (Bribery/Manhattan DA)

Department of Transportation/ Parking Violations Bureau

HIGHWAY ROBBERY. DOT supervisor and engineer conspired to perform private paving jobs by stealing city equipment and materials to complete the work. They also used 20 city employees who submitted false time cards to DOT and received a salary for time they were engaged in the private work. (Conspiracy; Grand Larceny; Offering a False Instrument for Filing/Brooklyn DA)

UPS. Nine Traffic Enforcement Agents falsified more than 100 parking summonses they had written and filed with DOT for processing and collection. (Falsifying Business Records; Offering a False Instrument for Filing/Manhattan DA)

PHANTOM OF BROADWAY. Two Traffic Enforcement Agents arrested for writing fraudulent traffic tickets. (Offering a False Instrument for Filing; Tampering with Public Records/Manhattan DA)

WEIGHT WATCHERS. Two employees in DOT's Traffic Intelligence Division accepted more than $100,000 to issue permits allowing overweight trucks to travel on city streets and bridges. (Bribe Receiving, Official Misconduct/Manhattan DA)

UP CHUCK. DOT assistant civil engineer solicited bribes to eliminate homeowners' sidewalk assessment charges. (Bribe Receiving/Queens DA)

UNCLE MILTIE. Inspector in DOT's sidewalk repair program solicited bribes from contractor in return for not issuing violations. (Bribe Receiving; Official Misconduct/Manhattan DA)

DISABLED. DOT employee sold two New York handicapped parking permits to individuals who were otherwise ineligible to obtain them. (Bribe Receiving; Official Misconduct/Brooklyn DA)

MOTOR DRIVE. DOT employees and private security guard at Bronx towpound charged with stealing parts from impounded vehicles. (Petit Larceny; Criminal Possession of Stolen Property/Bronx DA)

LED ASTRAY. Superintendent of Construction charged with misleading vendors in attempt to steer Staten Island Ferry repair contract to a Texas company. (Official Misconduct/Manhattan DA)

ROCKIN ROBIN. Employee of Parking Violations Bureau solicited and accepted bribe from undercover investigator in return for dismissing parking fines. (Bribe Receiving/Brooklyn DA)

JONES. PVB employee accepted cash in return for illegally dismissing more than $47,000 worth of summonses. (Grand Larceny; Bribe Receiving/Manhattan DA)

PALMS UP II. Traffic Enforcement Agent accepted bribes from motorists to insert an incorrect license plate number on tickets issued to them. (Bribe Receiving/Brooklyn DA)

THE SOUND OF MUSIC. Traffic Enforcement Agent accepted illegal payment to alter a license plate number on a summons. (Bribe Receiving/Manhattan DA)

TORRES. DEA employee illegally dismissed parking summonses by falsely representing to PVB that summonses were issued to DEA vehicle when actually issued to subject's husband's private vehicle. (Tampering with Public Records/Manhattan DA)

JACK IT UP. DOT employee submitted forged document to obtain dismissal of a parking summons. (Forgery/Brooklyn DA)

NYC TO NEWARK. Assistant bridge operator stole six DOT payroll checks and failed to disclose prior criminal history on employment applications. (Grand Larceny/Manhattan DA)

COLLECTION AGENCY. Former employee of a collection agency under contract with PVB to collect parking summons debts accepted payment from a debtor in exchange for settling parking fines owed. (Grand Larceny/Manhattan DA)

PVB CONTRACT. Former employee of a federal office under contract with the PVB illegally dismissed 167 parking summonses. (Tampering with Public Records; Computer Trespass/Manhattan DA)

PVB PRINTOUT. Employee of Health and Hospitals Corporation submitted an altered PVB printout in attempt to evade fines owed for parking violations. (Criminal Possession of Forged Instrument/Manhattan DA)

CHEM BANK. Temporary employee of Chemical Bank, a contract vendor of PVB, altered and negotiated two American Express money orders. (Forgery; Petit Larceny/Manhattan DA)

OH MY GUARD. Security guard for a PVB sub-contractor solicited illegal payments from three PVB respondents seeking to obtain a reduction in fines owed. (Robbery; Grand Larceny/SI DA)

CLAUDIO'S CAPER. An employee for a PVB sub-contractor illegally dismissed parking summonses issued to his father's vehicle. (Tampering With Public Records/Manhattan DA)

PVB COMPUTER. PVB employee made illegal entries in PVB computers to effect the dismissal of outstanding parking summonses owed by relatives. (Tampering With Public Records/ Queens DA)

BEEP BEEP. TEA solicited bribes in exchange for voiding a ticket and providing an improper permit. (Bribe Receiving/Manhattan DA)

WILLIE B. President of a paint company submitted a false financial statement to DOT concerning its relationship with another contract bidder in order to conceal the existence of a joint venture. (Offering a False Instrument for Filing/Brooklyn DA)

UNHOOK ME. Two Traffic Enforcement Agents solicited bribes from motorists to unhook the motorists' cars from tow trucks. (Bribe Receiving/Manhattan DA)

Department of Youth Services

WAGNER. Executive director of Vietnam Veterans organization, aided by a DYS employee, misappropriated government funds. (Theft of Public Money; Conspiracy to Defraud/U.S. Attorney for the Southern District of New York)

INDEX